SPIRITUAL NUTRITION

HEALTHY EATING FOR THE CHRISTIAN HEART

CHRISTINE PRESCOTT

WinePress **WP** Publishing

© 2009 by Christine Prescott. All rights reserved.

WinePress Publishing (PO Box 428, Enumclaw, WA 98022) functions only as book publisher. As such, the ultimate design, content, editorial accuracy, and views expressed or implied in this work are those of the author.

No part of this publication may be reproduced, stored in a retrieval system, or transmitted in any way by any means—electronic, mechanical, photocopy, recording, or otherwise—without the prior permission of the copyright holder, except as provided by USA copyright law.

Unless otherwise noted, all Scripture quotations are taken from the *Holy Bible: New International Version*®. NIV®. Copyright © 1973, 1978, 1984 by International Bible Society. Used by permission of Zondervan. All rights reserved.

Scripture references marked NRSB are taken from the *New Revised Standard Version of the Bible,* copyright © 1989 by the Division of Christian Education of the National Council of Churches of Christ in the United States of America. Used by permission.

This book contains advice and information relating to health. It is not intended to replace medical advice and should be used to supplement rather than replace regular care by your physician. Readers are encouraged to consult their physicians with specific questions and concerns.

ISBN 13: 978-1-60615-004-7
ISBN 10: 1-60615-004-9
Library of Congress Catalog Card Number: 2009922301

This is God's book.

Taste and see that the Lord is good.
—Psalm 34:8

Like newborn babies, crave pure spiritual milk,
so that by it you may grow up in your salvation,
now that you have tasted that the Lord is good.
—1 Peter 2:2–3

CONTENTS

Acknowledgments vii
Introduction. ix

1. Get Rid of Spiritual Flab 1
2. We Are What We Eat 5
3. Nutritional Pyramids 9
4. Fast Food 13
5. Prayer: The Water of Life 18
6. Bible Study: Spiritual Protein 34
7. Christian Fellowship: Carbohydrates for
    Spiritual Energy 52
8. Worship: Healthy Fats for a Healthy Heart. 66
9. Philippians 4:8: Spiritual Vitamins. 80
10. Missing Nutrients? 91
11. A Balanced Diet 103
12. More Nutrients with Less Effort. 109
13. I'm Ready to Make Some Changes—
    Now What Do I Do? 113

How to Make It Happen 119
    Ten Ways to Improve Your Spiritual Nutrition
    Meeting Our Minimum Spiritual Nutritional Needs
    My Personal Spiritual Meal Plan

A Week of Menu Ideas to Implement Your Spiritual
    Nutrition Needs
Spiritual Nutrition for Special Situations
  At Work
  Busy/Stressful Days
  When You Are Sick (includes What Are Your
    Spiritual Comfort Foods?)
  When Traveling

Resources 135
Endnotes 143

ACKNOWLEDGMENTS

Mary Jeanne Doyle, MS, RD, LD, reviewed the nutrition information in this book. She did her best to help me understand the intricacies of nutrition science. However, all responsibility for the nutrition information is mine alone. Any mistakes are mine.

Mary Jeanne has a Master's degree in nutrition. She is a registered dietitian and a member of the American Dietetics Association. She has over 20 years' experience in the nutrition field, working with adults and children. She has a private nutrition consulting practice in Missoula, Montana. Thanks, Mary Jeanne, for your expertise, your patience, your enthusiasm, and your encouragement.

Thanks, Kim Kinsinger of KDesigns Marketing, for designing my Spiritual Nutrition Pyramid. Your patience and creativity inspire me.

Thanks, Dallas and Karen Summerfield and Angela Seagler for reading the manuscript.

Thanks to the American Baptist Women of Oregon for being the guinea pigs for the original idea.

Thanks to the Nonfiction Critique group at the Oregon Christian Writers Conference in August 2007. This book is much better because of you.

Thanks, Joyce Ellis, for your ideas on my manuscript and for your great workshop at the Green Lake Writer's Conference, August 2008.

Thanks, Rachel Roberts, for welcoming me to your Bible study group.

Thanks, Angela and my husband, Dave, for being my advisors even though you probably got tired of hearing me go on and on about my book.

Thanks to everyone at WinePress Publishing Group who worked with me.

And thanks to everyone who gave words of encouragement. You helped me keep going.

To my parents, Dave, Samantha, and Milo. You nourish my heart.

INTRODUCTION

Oh, no—do we need another book that tells us to pray, read the Bible, and go to church? No, thanks. We already feel guilty, okay?

From television preachers, magazines, books, and the pulpit we hear that good Christians need to pray more—longer—better, know the Bible as if it were our best friend, and go joyfully to worship services every week (or more). We know we want to be better disciples of Jesus. But how?

Spiritual Nutrition shows how we can learn to pray, read the Bible, and be the followers of Jesus that we want to be by thinking of what we need for our spirits as food. And we know how much we think about food! Comparing what we know about food with spiritual principles gives us a unique way to understand and meet our craving for spiritual health. This book contains practical, fun ideas to help us feel less guilty and more excited about our relationship with Jesus.

GET RID OF SPIRITUAL FLAB

CHAPTER 1

> Stand firm. Let nothing move you.
> —1 Corinthians 15:58

Raise your hand if you want to have a flabby spiritual life. The flab on our bodies is soft and easily shaken. In the same way, spiritual flab makes a soft, weak Christian who is easily influenced and cannot endure the shaking that life doles out day by day.

You and I don't want to be spiritually flabby. We want to be Christians who stand firm, who are vital with the life of Jesus Christ and effective in doing God's will every day in every circumstance.

Just as the flab in our physical bodies will only go away through consistently healthy eating and exercise, our spiritual flab can only be removed through a good spiritual diet and exercise that becomes a part of our daily lives.

At times, all of us feel that something is lacking in our spiritual lives. Usually we just wait for the mood to pass. Sometimes we talk to our friends or our pastor or try to find help in a spiritual book. What if, instead, we could take an active approach to restore our spiritual zeal? What if we could help ourselves eliminate spiritual flab and the weakness it causes in our spiritual lives?

We can. Spiritual health is not different from physical health. Some physical problems require the help of a medical professional. But we can prevent or treat many of our physical problems ourselves by rest, exercise, adjusting our diet, and trying to lower our stress levels at home and at work. Some spiritual problems require the help of a trained Christian counselor. However, many times the malaise of our spirits can be treated by the application of good spiritual nutrition.

It is easy to see and easy to feel the flab on our bodies. The flab of our spirits is harder to detect. Maybe right now you feel spiritually blah; you have a sense that something isn't right in your relationship with God. Diagnosis of the source of our spiritual weakness can be difficult. Understanding where our spiritual lives need building up requires courage and openness to the voice of the Holy Spirit and the voices of wise Christian friends.

Maybe you already have an idea about how you need to improve spiritually. Maybe you're not sure. Maybe you think your spiritual life is great. If so, just remember the many people who are shocked to discover that they have cancer, diabetes, or heart disease when they feel perfectly healthy.

This book does not present a thirty-day magic spiritual flab eradication program. It is not a guilt book, written with a finger pointed at you. This book is a practical guide to help you diagnose and treat the sources of your spiritual weakness and develop lifelong habits to maintain spiritual health.

The five core spiritual nutrients are compared with the body's counterpart nutrients. The sections on water, protein, carbohydrates, healthy fats, and vitamins explain these nutrients' functions in our bodies and the healthiest foods to eat for each nutrient. Because most of us eat fast foods, tips are given for wise choices of fast foods in each nutrient category.

The corresponding spiritual nutrient section describes the nutrient and its importance in our Christian lives. Most of us are busy and often find our day packed with activities so "fast food" (quick) spiritual practices are suggested. The "fast food" options need to be balanced with more nourishing (more time consuming) practices in each area. Nourishing activities are described as well as practical ways to discover the time to do them. Gray boxes describe specific, easy, and fun ideas to try.

The nutrients in food and how those nutrients are like the nutrients we need for our spirits are discussed in each chapter. To avoid confusion the ~~~ symbol will identify a discussion of food. The 🕊 will denote a discussion of spiritual nutrients.

As you are reading, mark ideas that you would like to try or places where you feel the Holy Spirit's nudge (or even kick). You may want to write these points in a notebook (with the page number in the book) so that you can look for and write down ideas for addressing any need or problem.

Each chapter ends with questions to help you identify where you are doing well and areas that you may need to work on. Again, practical ideas are given to help encourage you to build up your spiritual health. These questions make *Spiritual Nutrition* easy to use with small groups. Successes can be celebrated and problems explored together in loving support.

To make improving spiritual health even more practical, at the end of the book is a section titled "How to Make it Work." The first list is "Ten Ways to Improve Your Spiritual Nutrition." What is one thing on that list that you could easily do every day? "A Week of Menu Ideas" helps you practice many ways to incorporate good spiritual nutrition in every part of your day. You will find some ideas that will be just right for you.

SPIRITUAL NUTRITION

"Spiritual Nutrition for Special Situations" has specific, easy ways to maintain spiritual health at work, on busy/stressful days, when you are sick, and when traveling.

Ready to improve your spiritual health? Then let's go.

CHAPTER 2

WE ARE WHAT WE EAT

> [Jesus'] disciples urged him, "Rabbi, eat something." But he said to them, "I have food to eat that you know nothing about."[1]
>
> —John 4:31–2

Several months after I started my law practice I realized that when I came home from work I crashed on the couch for the rest of the evening, exhausted. What happened to all my energy? One afternoon as I lay on the couch channel surfing and feeling drained, I found a show that was promoting the book, *Arnold's Bodybuilding for Women.* Maybe bodybuilding would help me have more energy after work. So I bought the book, some weights, and started bodybuilding.

When I was asked to speak at a state women's conference, I could speak on any subject I wanted. Perhaps because I was thinking about the relationship between nutrition and my bodybuilding efforts, I started thinking about spiritual nutrition. Can spiritual health be compared to physical health? Can an understanding of the nutrients in our food and the way these nutrients help our bodies and cells grow, fight off disease,

SPIRITUAL NUTRITION

and enable us to live energetically help us to understand how to be spiritually healthy?

We are a people who are obsessed with food. Many of us seem to move from diet to diet in an attempt to create our idea of the perfect body. There is no shortage of diets from which to choose. There are diets named for people: Atkins. Jenny Craig. There are diets named for places: South Beach. Mediterranean. There are diets named for the food one can eat: Grapefruit. Cabbage soup. Subway. There is even the "No Diet" diet. Nearly every magazine in the checkout lane at the grocery store proclaims that between its covers is the perfect exercise program and a diet that is "guaranteed to work."

As I started thinking about comparing physical nutrition with spiritual nutrition, I wondered, *What is nutrition, anyway?* One dictionary defined nutrition as "the process of being nourished." (Not a big help!) Nourishment is "that which supports life and growth in a living organism." The words *nutrition, nourishment,* and *nutrient* ("something that nourishes") come from the Latin *nutrire,* "to feed." What we feed on—our food—supports life and growth in our bodies and minds. What we feed on—our spiritual food—helps our spirits live and grow in Jesus.

A healthy diet includes a balance of protein, carbohydrates, fat, vitamins, minerals, water, and exercise. All the nutrients work together to ensure physical health. What about spiritual health? What nutrients—those things that support life and growth—do we need for optimal *spiritual* nutrition? How do the spiritual nutrients compare with the nutrients we need in our food?

1. The most important spiritual nutrient—as important as water is to our bodies—is prayer. Prayer maintains our connection with the living, active God. Prayer is the source of our power to act for Jesus in the world.

2. We also need to study the Bible to help us grow, just as protein helps our physical bodies grow. Bible study maintains our connection with God through God's written Word and helps us know how God wants us to live in the world.
3. The right amount of time spent with other Christians gives us the energy to live our lives for Jesus just as the right amount of carbohydrates gives our bodies the energy to do the tasks we demand of them.
4. In the same way that healthy fats can help our hearts resist the build-up of heart attack and stroke-inducing plaque, when we come together in worship we create health in our spiritual hearts.
5. We need to fill our minds with what is good, true, and pure just as we need vitamins in our diet. Filling our minds with what is good keeps us looking to Jesus no matter what our outward circumstances may be.

Love, disciplined giving, and service are additional nutrients we may need and are the exercise in our spiritual lives. All the spiritual nutrients work together to help our spiritual lives function in the best possible way.

This book does not present a formula. Each person's spiritual nutritional requirements will be different because each person's life and relationship to God is unique.

We practice good spiritual nutrition not just for ourselves, but also for the church, the body of Christ. Our local church can exist by meeting together once a week. But we will not be a vibrant, living, growing, exciting church that makes a difference in our community unless each individual practices good spiritual nutrition. We must, as individual Christians, maintain a balance of all the spiritual nutrients in our lives. We then bring our spiritual health to our church to follow Jesus Christ together. A spiritually-healthy church—made up of spiritually-healthy individuals—will live and grow, reproducing itself in the world.

Do you feel spiritually strong and vibrant or spiritually flabby and tired? Do you feel like something is missing in your relationship with God? If so, you may be short on one of the elements of spiritual nutrition. After I had begun a sermon series on spiritual nutrition, a woman came up to me with a grin and the list of spiritual nutrients. She pointed to one: "I knew something was wrong with my spiritual life but I didn't know what. I was missing *this* part." Adjust your spiritual nutrition and see what a difference it can make to you and to your church.

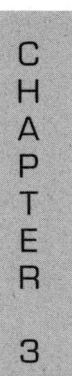

NUTRITIONAL PYRAMIDS

CHAPTER 3

Listen, listen to me, and eat what is good, and your soul will delight in the richest of fare.
—Isaiah 55:2

Food pyramids

Since 1894 the United States government has provided tools to help people make healthy food choices that are based on the most current nutrition science.

In 1941, the Food and Nutrition Board of the National Academy of Sciences issued the first Recommended Daily Allowances (RDA) for food. They recommended daily intakes for calories and for nine essential nutrients.

In 1943, the United States Department of Agriculture (USDA) issued the "Basic Seven" food guide to help Americans eat well within the limitations of food rationing during World War II.[2]

The USDA released the first graphic food pyramid in 1992.[3] This is the food pyramid that most of us recognize.

SPIRITUAL NUTRITION

The purpose of food pyramids is to help people choose nutritious foods for a healthy diet. Food pyramids have been developed for various ethnic groups. Several countries have their own dietary guidelines that differ from the current food pyramid in use in the United States, MyPyramid.[4]

MyPyramid

The current USDA Food Pyramid: "MyPyramid: Steps to a Healthier You" was introduced in 2005 (*www.mypyramid.com*). A stylized figure runs up steps at the side of a large triangle made up of smaller triangles of various colors. The colors represent the different food groups: grains, vegetables, fruits, milk, and meat & beans. MyPyramid is the first dietary tool to include physical exercise as an important part of a healthy lifestyle.

The name "MyPyramid" indicates that the guidelines are based on the needs of each individual. The "MyPyramid Plan" on *www.mypyramid.gov* is an interactive menu-planning tool designed to make it easy for each individual to meet his or her nutritional needs.[5]

Using "MyPyramid Plan" one enters one's height, weight, gender, and physical activity to find out how many calories to eat each day. A listing of the servings of foods needed each day in each food group is included.

NUTRITIONAL PYRAMIDS

A Spiritual Nutrition Pyramid

A balanced spiritual diet, as I describe it, can be drawn as a pyramid.

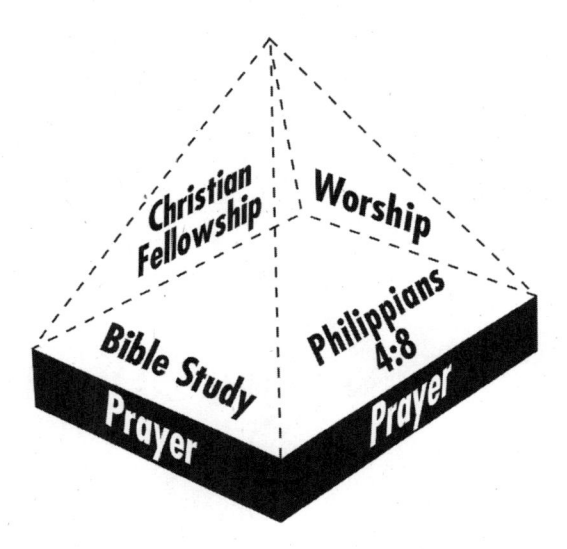

The base of the Spiritual Nutrition Pyramid is prayer, anchoring the other nutrients. The four sides of the pyramid are worship, Bible study, Christian fellowship, and Philippians 4:8 (thinking on good things). The dotted lines on the sides of this pyramid indicate that the sides are not rigidly divided but blend into each other.

As in MyPyramid, in the Spiritual Nutrition Pyramid all the elements are necessary and work together. One missing or insufficient element will hinder effective spiritual nutrition; the pyramid will be weak or may even collapse. In MyPyramid, optimal health results from physical activity in combination with a healthy diet. We will consider how love, giving, and service are exercises that are essential for good spiritual health.

FAST FOOD

CHAPTER 4

> Eat the meat roasted over the fire, along with bitter herbs, and bread made without yeast. . . . This is how you are to eat it: with your cloak tucked into your belt, your sandals on your feet and your staff in your hand. Eat it in haste.
> —Exodus 12:8, 11

Fast food for our bodies

What is your favorite fast food?

Mine? I like fresh cut, just-out-of-the-deep-fryer, greasy French fries. Would I want to live on them? I think so, when I start eating them. But after about half a basketful, when I'm starting to feel a little queasy from the grease, I know I wouldn't want to make French fries my diet staple. While they taste good, French fries have lots of fat and salt and little nutrition to help my body function properly.

SPIRITUAL NUTRITION

If you haven't seen the movie *Supersize Me*, see it. A reporter decided to eat all his meals at McDonald's for a month and supersize his meal if he was asked to do so. After a few weeks, his team of doctors tried to get him to stop because his blood pressure was so high that he was in imminent danger of dying from a stroke or heart attack. When he stopped at the end of the month, he found that he had become addicted to the fat and sugar he was eating in his fast-food-only diet.

What is fast food?

Fast food or convenience food is food that is quick, inexpensive, and easily available. Fast food may be food to eat on the go from a restaurant or sidewalk stand or packaged food from the supermarket that is ready to heat and eat. Prepackaged food will often have preservatives and other chemicals to increase shelf life.

Fast food is easy to get on the go or to prepare when time is short, but we need to be aware of what we are eating. Fast food can be high in fat, especially artery-clogging trans fat and saturated fat, salt, sugar, and calories.

Although some restaurants that serve fast food claim to cook their foods in a healthy way, the buyer has no control over how the food is really cooked. Not being health inspectors with testing kits, we just unwrap the food and eat it.

What—no fries?

Choose wisely. At fast-food restaurants, order a children's meal. You usually don't have to show your ID or a small child to order a child-sized meal. I often order a small hamburger, plain, cooked with no salt. It arrives fresh and hot because it has to be cooked to order. I put my own ketchup on the burger. For breakfast I order an Egg McMuffin without cheese. Yes, I have to wait and sometimes I have to send it back because the cheese is on it. But when the cheeseless sandwich arrives it is hot and has less fat than the same sandwich with a slice of processed cheese. Order small fries instead of a large order. Share with a friend.

Choose water, not soda. Choose meat that is grilled or baked instead of deep-fried.

Balance less nutritious choices with better choices. If you (or I) must have the French fries, we can balance out the fat, salt, and calories by ordering water to drink, a plain hamburger, or a green salad with fat-free dressing on the side. Such a meal sounds boring but our bodies will thank us.

In grocery stores we can find fried chicken, pizza, and fried potatoes in the deli. Better fast food choices are the salad bar (with low fat dressing) or fresh packaged salads, hard-boiled eggs, bags of carrot or celery sticks, and bagged salad greens.

Being smart about fast food takes more time. But for our health, being smart about fast food is, well, smart.

Spiritual fast food

Just like fast food that we eat, spiritual fast food is quick and easy. A quick prayer, a glance at a devotional for the day, listening to a religious television program while we do household chores or a Christian radio station in the car are all examples of spiritual fast food.

Like fast food, spiritual fast food gives us some spiritual nutrition. But the danger of spiritual fast food is that we will use it as a replacement for spiritual nutrition that takes more time but leads us into a deeper relationship with Jesus Christ.

To achieve our best spiritual health we must balance quick spiritual practices with practices that take us longer to do. For

SPIRITUAL NUTRITION

example, if the beginning of our day is rushed, we can glance at the devotional in the morning. At lunch or in the evening we can study the Scripture passage the devotional is based on and have a time of prayer. We can balance watching a television worship service with attending a worship service during the week.

In each spiritual nutrition section—prayer, Bible study, worship, Christian fellowship, and practicing Philippians 4:8—ideas will be given for healthy spiritual fast food choices and how to balance those choices with spiritual nutrition choices that are more nourishing.

PRAYER: THE WATER OF LIFE

Chapter 5

"Those who drink the water that I will give them will never be thirsty. The water that I will give will become in them a spring of water gushing up to eternal life." The woman said to him, "Sir, give me this water . . ."

—John 4:14–15, NRSB

Prayer is not given us as a burden to be borne, or an irksome duty to fulfil, but to be a joy and power to which there is no limit.

—*The Kneeling Christian*

Our spirits' need for prayer

I once worked in an office where the unpredictable rages of the boss created a tense, soul-shriveling environment. Without warning he would call an employee and scream, "You are stupid and worthless. You're fired." Ten minutes later he would call back and contritely say, "Never mind. I didn't mean it."

Every morning before I started work and at the beginning of the afternoon, I sat at my desk and prayed for God to create a force field of love and protection around me. Each prayer was like a deep, cool drink of water on a trek through a barren desert.

Our bodies' need for water

- Water is the most important nutrient in our bodies. Sixty percent or more of the human body is made up of water.
- Our bodies require water to stay alive. Water helps carry nutrients from our food and oxygen to our organs and is the medium for the chemical processes in our bodies. Water also carries away the waste products our bodies produce.
- Dehydration, when the body lacks enough water to function properly, can be a serious condition. A person can die within days without water.
- Every day we need to replenish the water our bodies lose through perspiration, breathing, and the excretion of urine and feces. People need different amounts of water, depending on factors such as the temperature outside, whether they are exercising or are losing water because of illness or medication.
- The human body can get the water it needs from any food except oils. Water, milk, juice, tea, and fruits and vegetables have the most water content.

SPIRITUAL NUTRITION

Prayer is water for our spirits. Our spirits require prayer to live. Without prayer our spiritual lives become dry and shriveled and dead.

As followers of Jesus, the Holy Spirit lives in us (John 14:15–24). When we pray, our hearts and minds open for the power of the Holy Spirit to flow through us and into the world. Prayer connects us with the power of God.

The ingredients of effective prayer

Effective prayer, whether fast food prayer or nourishing prayer includes:

>PRAISING GOD
>
>THANKSGIVING
>
>PETITION: making our requests known to God (Philippians 4:6).

Other important parts of prayer are

>CONFESSION: admitting our sins to God, and
>
>INTERCESSION: praying for the needs of others.

Sometimes the difference between praise and thanksgiving is unclear. Consider this letter that my sweet niece might send me:

> Dear Aunt Chris,
> Thank you for the birthday present. You are the best aunt in the history of the world. Thank you for being so special.
> Love, your sweet niece

She is thanking me for a present, giving me praise for being a perfect example of aunt-ness and is giving me thanks and praise for being special to her. Generally speaking, we give praise for qualities and thanks for gifts. Yes, sometimes we give praise to someone for his or her gifts. Thanksgiving and praise can and often do meld. However, it is important to praise God for God's attributes—such as God's love, grandeur, power, the perfection of wisdom—when we begin our prayers. After all, this is God we are praying to, not a human being. When we praise God we remember that we are not God. We stand before God in awe at the greatness of God and the greatness of God's love for us.

What do I say when I pray?

We can be silent when we pray. Sitting quietly in the presence of God is a powerful source of spiritual nourishment.

In our words, we pray the elements shown above: praise, thanksgiving, petition, confession, and intercession.

What should we pray for? Is there anything too insignificant to include in a prayer? My favorite prayer request one Sunday morning was from a child: "Please pray for my fish. He has ich." As this child knew, if we care about something, God cares about it. The book of Hebrews instructs us to "approach the throne of grace with confidence, so that we may receive mercy and find grace to help us in our time of need" (Hebrew 4:16).

Because we live in a results-driven world, we often need to remind ourselves that the effectiveness of prayer is not measured by whether we get what we want. Remember, thanksgiving and praise are part of prayer. Prayer is not a grocery list. Prayer is our connection to the life-giving and life-sustaining power of God.

We can pray alone. We can pray with our family members and friends. When we pray in groups, such as prayer during worship services or prayer in small groups, we are physically connected with the body of Christ, the church, as we come into God's presence.

SPIRITUAL NUTRITION

Do I have to pray in a certain position?

There are no legalistic rules for prayer positions. Try kneeling or sitting on the floor or in a chair. Sometimes you may even feel like praying face down. Try various postures and see what seems to work best for you, spiritually and physically.

Different times will call for different ways of praying. There have been times when I was so overwhelmed by the power of God that my only response was to put my face to the ground and cry. Kneeling, if we can, reminds us that we are in the presence of our Lord. Let your heart speak.

What is the best way to pray?

The "best" way to pray is the way in which we come to God honestly, with humility, and with courage.

Fast food prayer

I define fast food prayer as a quick prayer for something we want like a parking space or a moment of quiet. These quick prayers are prayers. But these prayers are more like the cups of water a marathon runner grabs from a table during a race. She gulps a swallow, pours some over her head, and tosses the rest away. She gets some water for hydration or to cool her body but not enough to sustain life.

Fast food prayer is not bad in itself. Sometimes quick prayers are the most appropriate prayers. Brother Lawrence, the pot-scrubbing monk, writes in *The Practice of the Presence of God* that it is important to take brief moments during the day as we do our work to adore and praise God (what he calls "interior acts of adoration" which are "very pleasing to God").

Quick prayers provide us with some spiritual sustenance. However, to nourish our minds and hearts for growth, quick prayers must grow out of times we set aside from our day to spend in God's presence.

PRAYER: THE WATER OF LIFE

When I was attending law school, I rarely prayed. (I rarely attended worship services or studied the Bible, either.) After I graduated, I began to spend time in prayer and Bible study to decide if the phrase "Christian lawyer" was an oxymoron for me. During this time, a professor I had known when I was growing up was in the hospital, dying. I felt certain that I was supposed to visit him. My heart was fearful: What would I say? Would he even remember me? As I approached the street where the hospital was located, I prayed, wishing that I wouldn't have to visit. I prayed, "God, if you want me to visit, make a parking space for me." I was certain there would not be a space, as the on-street parking was very limited. To my surprise (sort of), there was a space just the length of my car in front of the hospital. When I got to his room, his wife, who had been acting as gatekeeper, had just left. So I went in and although he was tired, he seemed genuinely glad to see me. We had a good conversation. He died several weeks later.

My time with God in prayer and Bible study opened my heart to hearing God's voice. Obeying God's voice showed me how God would make a way for me to do what was asked of me. Fast food prayers that come out of longer times of prayer lead us to a deeper relationship with God.

Good Fast Food Prayers: A Diet Plan for a Week

To practice using nutritious fast food prayers, try this schedule:

When is a busy time of your day? Choose this time to practice nutritious fast food praying. Each day at about the same time, practice one type of prayer. As you gain confidence, you can pray in any way that is appropriate for the moment.

SPIRITUAL NUTRITION

MONDAY: Let your prayers be of thanksgiving. Give thanks for the beauty around you, that you are physically able to work out, for your family, that your car works, that you have a job, or anything you can thank God for.

TUESDAY: Give praise to God. Tell God how great, how wonderful, and how glorious he is.

WEDNESDAY: Pray a prayer of intercession. Pray for your spouse, children, friends, your boss, the person in the cubicle next to you, the bus driver, the mail carrier, or a stranger you pass on the sidewalk during the day. Pray that God will bless them, that they will have a good day, that God will be with them to help them with anything that is troubling them. You can also pray for someone you know who is sick or having a difficult time.

THURSDAY: Pray a prayer of petition, asking God for something you want. Sometimes these are the only prayers that we think to pray. Prayers of petition need to be balanced with prayers of praise, thanksgiving, and intercession, which is why we practice them first.

FRIDAY: In the morning, before you go out, choose your prayer for the day: thanksgiving, praise, or intercession. If you attend worship on a Saturday, pray the "Saturday" prayer below.

SATURDAY: Pray for the worship leaders at the church you will be attending the next day. Pray that God will speak through them. Pray that God will speak to the hearts of all those who will attend the service.

Now you have a choice of fast food prayers that will nourish you until you are able to pray for a longer time.

Nourishing prayer

Sometimes we spend hours on a meal for our family and friends. We carefully plan the meal, search for recipes, buy the ingredients, lovingly make the meal, and present it using our best dishes, tablecloth, napkins, and a centerpiece. Nourishing prayer is like such a meal.

Ways to practice nourishing prayer

Praying a verse of Scripture

Choose a passage of Scripture: a parable of Jesus, a story (such as David and Goliath) or several verses from any book of the Bible. Pray that the Holy Spirit will show you what you need to learn from the Scripture you have chosen. Read the passage quietly and sit in silence. Pray and read the verse once a day for several weeks and listen for the word God will speak to you.

I tried this prayer and reading to help me resolve a question in my life. Should I accept a call to a particular church that had fired its last pastor? Because the time was near Christmas, the passage I chose was Matthew 1:18–21, where Joseph finds out that his fiancée, Mary, is pregnant. He wants to quietly divorce her. God tells Joseph, "Do not be afraid to take Mary home as your wife."

I read the verses every night without trying to coax an answer from them. After two weeks, the answer I heard was, "Don't be afraid to go."

Silent prayer

We should also practice times of wordless prayer, simply sitting and enjoying being in God's presence.

SPIRITUAL NUTRITION

When we are silent we can hear. Prayer is often defined as listening to God. Have you ever been in the presence of someone who talked and talked and talked...? You "couldn't get a word in edgewise." God desires that we sit silently and listen as well as speak in our times of prayer.

> **A Prayer Suggestion**
>
> "As I enter into prayer today, I ask the Lord to open my lips to speak to him but first for an open ear to listen to him."
>
> from pray-as-you-go podcast
> 11 Aug 2008

Grace before meals

When we say a prayer before our meals (which we call "grace"), we remember to thank God for his blessings of food and for our table companions. While table grace takes little time, it teaches us to remember that God's goodness has given us everything we have.

Have you ever seen a family bow in prayer before a meal at a restaurant? When I do, I feel that I am in the presence of a holy moment. Table grace is a good witness to others nearby when we eat out.

Prayer with other Christians

The church in which you worship may have times when people gather together for prayer. You can pray with friends before a Bible study or book study group. If there is a special need in the congregation or the community, invite others to gather together to pray for the need or the individual. Pray with others for your schools, the poor in your community, or your church leadership.

PRAYER: THE WATER OF LIFE

Times we spend praying with others are special times, not only for Christian fellowship but also to hear others pray and learn about the needs of others for which we can pray during the week.

How do I learn to pray?

One of the best ways to learn to pray is by listening to the prayers of others. When we feel the power of someone's prayer, we can imitate the words and make them our own. When I was in seminary, we prayed at the start of every class (a shock after law school!). One of my classmates was from Nigeria. When he prayed for God to heal another, he called on "The Great Physician." He would pray, "Jesus, You are the Great Physician. You know exactly what is wrong with his body. We ask you to reach into his body, into the places that need healing and heal them." I could visualize the hand of Jesus reaching into the person's body and touching exactly the place where healing was needed. I have prayed this prayer many times for the healing of others and for myself as I visualized Jesus' fingers touching the diseased parts of the body. My husband, Dave, often prays this prayer when we pray together for the healing of another.

We can also learn to pray by reading written collections of prayers such as the book of Psalms in the Bible. Ask your pastor or Christian friend about other books with collections of prayers that they may be willing to loan or recommend.

We can learn to pray from studying the prayers in the Bible (including the psalms). As an example, we will look at **Jacob's prayer** in Genesis 32:9–12.

SPIRITUAL NUTRITION

Background

Jacob heard that his estranged older brother, Esau, was on his way to meet Jacob. Jacob had alienated his brother, Esau, by pretending to be Esau (dressing like Esau and giving their father meat) to cheat Esau out of his inheritance. Esau was so angry with Jacob that he wanted to kill Jacob. So Jacob ran away to live with his uncle Laban and stayed there for twenty years. Now Jacob has run away with Rachel, Leah, and their children to Gilead. Jacob hears that Esau is coming to meet him with four hundred men.

Read Genesis 32:1–23

How scared was Jacob? What did he think Esau was going to do? (v. 7–8)

What did Jacob pray for?

What did Jacob do after his prayer?

What happened when Esau met Jacob? (33:1–4)

PRAYER: THE WATER OF LIFE

Jacob's prayer

- Prayer is a first resort not a last resort. After Jacob hears that Esau is coming, he divides the people with him into two groups (v. 7–8). Then Jacob prays.
- At the beginning of his prayer, Jacob reminds himself and God that God has told him to return to his own land and that God has promised to be with him.
- Jacob admits who he is before God (v. 10). In his dealings with others, Jacob goes after what he wants regardless of the effect on others. But before God, Jacob admits who he is. Jacob comes to God with empty hands. He says, "I am not worthy of the least of all the steadfast love and all the faithfulness that you have shown to your servant." Because God is love and God is faithful, Jacob has prospered. Jacob has not earned anything—God has given it all to him because of who God is.
- Jacob makes his request to God. He tells God that he is afraid of Esau (v. 11). He asks God to save him from being killed by Esau. "Save me, I pray, from the hand of my brother, Esau, for I am afraid of him."
- Jacob ends his prayer by reminding God and himself of God's promise, "to make your offspring as the sand of the sea, which cannot be counted" (v. 12). Jacob begins his prayer with God's promise and ends with God's promise to do good and not harm.

After Jacob prays, he acts, taking animals from his herds as a gift for Esau that will go ahead of Jacob and his family. Because of his prayer, Jacob had absolute faith in what God had promised.

SPIRITUAL NUTRITION

Lessons from Jacob's prayer

- **Prayer is a first resort,** not something we do after we have tried everything else.
- **We praise God.**

  - When we begin our prayer, we declare that God loves us and is faithful to us and that all we have belongs to God and is due to God's love for us. We praise God for who God is.
  - As Christians, we thank God for his faithfulness in remembering and fulfilling his promise to send the Messiah, Jesus, to us. We can do nothing on our own to make God love us. God has always loved us. God loved the "cosmos"—the world—so much that he made the way for every person to come into his presence and pray by of the death and resurrection of his Son, Jesus Christ (John 3:16).

- **We tell God our feelings.** Why do we have to tell God how we feel? God surely knows how we feel. God wants us to express our feelings. Sometimes we are too proud to admit to others or to ourselves that we are scared or hurt or angry. If we have a personal relationship with God, we want to talk to God as a friend about what is on our hearts. We want to share our deepest feelings. Sometimes we need to say how we feel so that we know how we feel.
- After we have praised God and told God how we feel **we make our requests.**

We learn from the prayer of Jacob to come to God confessing our total reliance on God, acknowledging that God loves

PRAYER: THE WATER OF LIFE

us and is faithful. We tell God how we feel and then make our requests. Then we act in faith on God's promises.

What have you learned from Jacob's prayer that you will put into practice in your own prayers?

Water is essential for life.

Prayer is like water to our spiritual lives. It takes more effort to include prayer in our lives than it does to get enough water into our bodies. We must be intentional about including prayer in our busy lives, especially nourishing prayer.

It is by prayer that our hearts and minds open to the flow of the Holy Spirit through us enabling us to live for God. Prayer connects us with the power of God. Andrew Murray, South African evangelist and preacher, says that in prayer, we take hold of God's strength.[6]

Time spent in stillness before God refreshes our hearts, maintains and deepens our relationship to God, and gives us the space to listen to God's voice. When we have a request of God, preparation, humility, confession, and honesty lead us to a certainty of God's love and empower our requests.

Prayer is life.

SPIRITUAL NUTRITION

Do you have enough prayer in your diet?

How many times have you prayed in the last three days? ____
   Describe your prayers:

   What did you pray for?

   Where did you pray? _____
   Were you distracted or interrupted? _____
   Did you pray as much as you wanted to? _____
   Did you pray as often as you intended to? _____
   If not, why not? _____
   Do you have a special time to pray? _____
      When is it? _____
   Do you have a special place to pray? _____
      When is it? _____

   Having a special place to pray at home can help your mind quickly settle down for a time of prayer.

   What helps you pray (for example music, a candle, a special chair)?

   What distractions to prayer do you need to prepare for?

BIBLE STUDY: SPIRITUAL PROTEIN

CHAPTER 6

> [God's] Word is lively and inexhaustible, for God himself lives in it.
>
> —Dietrich Bonhoeffer

Our spirits' need for Bible study

My first pastorate was in a tiny town of 165 people in Northeastern Oregon. Many of the young adults who had grown up in the church still lived in the town. They now had families and most of them were not attending any church.

At the request of these young adults, we started a beginning Bible study, Bible study 101, Bible study as if one had never heard of the Bible. (Lesson One: This is the Bible. It has two parts.) We met every Monday evening except for the third Monday of the month, when the members of the group attended meetings of city boards and committees.

If the pages of the Bible had been food, these young adults would have eaten every page. They were starving to learn and

BIBLE STUDY: SPIRITUAL PROTEIN

to experience God's Word. It was thrilling to hear their questions, share their excitement, and see them grow. Although each couple had children, childcare was never a problem. The six couples and one single man came ready to devour the Bible.

As they grew in their faith through their study together, they began to bring their families to worship services. The women organized and taught the Vacation Bible School that summer and several of them helped in the primary Sunday school.

The protein in our food helps our physical bodies grow. The study of God's Word, the Bible, is our source of spiritual protein. Through the study of the Bible, we grow in Christ.

Our bodies' need for protein

- The proteins we eat in our food are used to manufacture enzymes, which speed up chemical reactions in the body.
- Protein helps our bodies repair cells and make new cells.[7]
- Proteins are used to make the neurotransmitters that help us think, move, and interact with the world through our senses.[8]
- Nine of the twenty amino acids that our bodies need cannot be made by our bodies and must be supplied from the protein in the food we eat. Therefore, we need to eat protein every day.
- Protein is used for tissue growth. Lack of protein causes poor growth in children.
- A balanced diet will give most people an adequate amount of protein. It is important to choose a variety of protein-rich foods.

SPIRITUAL NUTRITION

- Good sources of protein are lean meat and poultry, beans and lentils, nuts, seeds, fish, eggs, and fat-free or low fat milk, cheese, and yogurt. (For specific food suggestions see *mypyramid.gov* "Inside the Pyramid" meat & beans and milk food groups.)
- Soybeans, tofu, and veggie burgers also supply protein in our diets.
- Some of the above protein sources can contain too much fat for our diets. As a general rule, we should eat lean meat (without visible fat), remove the skin from poultry, choose low-fat or fat-free cheeses and milk products, and be careful of the portions we eat.

What about the protein in fast foods?

Meats and cheeses in fast food are often high in fat.

- Choose broiled chicken or fish instead of deep-fried varieties. As much as it hurts (I love extra crispy), take the skin and the breading off the fried chicken.
- Choose a small burger.
- Choose low-fat milk instead of milkshakes.
- Consider skipping the cheese on sandwiches, wraps, burgers, and fries.
- If you are having pizza, go easy on the cheese. Get a low-fat kind of meat, like Canadian bacon, and lots of veggies.
- If you make your meal a salad at a salad bar, put beans, sunflower seeds, and a small portion of shredded cheese on your salad.
- Order a Gardenburger® or Boca burger instead of a hamburger.

BIBLE STUDY: SPIRITUAL PROTEIN

What is the Bible?

Christians call the Bible "the Word of God" or "God's Word." We call the Bible "God's Word" because it contains the words spoken from God to our hearts. The apostle Paul tells Timothy that the Scriptures are "God-breathed" (2 Timothy 3:16). Spiritual life without God's Word will be based on the words we hear from others or in our own minds. We need to study God's Word so that we know *God's* mind.

Studying God's Word leads to understanding God's Word (Psalm 119:27, 34, 104, 130, 144). Understanding God's Word helps us to keep to the straight path. In *The Hobbit*, Bilbo and the dwarves are warned to go through the dark woods by staying on the path. Gandalf tells them, "Don't leave the path." But they get hungry and discouraged and go off the path in search of a feast, thinking that it will be easy to find the path again. However, they only go further and further away from the path until they are hopelessly lost (and have a close encounter with giant spiders). Without knowing God's Word, we, too, will stray off the path and meet giant spiders of our own.

God's Word also becomes our light. (The refrigerator light that helps us see what we're about to eat?) The psalmist calls God's Word "a lamp to my feet and a light for my path" (Psalm 119:105). Without the light of God's Word, we are like people with no flashlight walking in the forest at night. The edge of a cliff could be right in front of us and we would not see it even as we walked off the edge.

As we walk straight on God's path we have peace, the peace that we all long for. "Great peace have they who love your law, and nothing can make them stumble" (Psalm 119:165).

SPIRITUAL NUTRITION

How is Bible study like the protein in our diets?

The first Bible study I remember was in Oregon at a junior high summer camp set in an old-growth forest near Mt. Hood. Each morning in groups of four with an adult leader we would go off into the woods for Bible study. Our group walked down the hill from the lodge, across the old wood bridge to the river. On the first morning, our adult leader gave us instructions to ask about a passage: "What does it say? What does it mean? What does it mean to me?" (Later I learned that this method is called "inductive Bible study.") As I sat by the sparkling Zig Zag River with my Bible and notebook open beside me, I understood for the first time that studying the Bible would help me grow as a Christian in my everyday life. The words of the Bible weren't just for my head but for my heart and my life at home and school.

The protein in our food helps our physical bodies grow and function properly. God's Word, the Bible, is our source of spiritual growth. We begin our spiritual lives as newborn babies who need the spiritual milk of the Word to grow (1 Peter 2:2). Children who do not get enough protein fail to grow properly. To grow into mature believers we must take in our protein—the Word of God as it has been given to us in the Bible.

The study of God's Word is not just an intellectual exercise. The purpose of understanding God's Word is to make the Word a part of our lives every day in everything we do, say, and think. As Dietrich Bonhoeffer teaches, "Daily, quiet reflection on the Word of God as it applies to me (even if only for a few minutes)" is a gift that keeps my life steady, my heart peaceful and can be "a source of health and strength."[9]

We study the Bible so that we can understand God's mind and God's heart and how God wants us to live our lives in the world.

BIBLE STUDY: SPIRITUAL PROTEIN

There are lots of versions of the Bible. Which one should I use?

Does the version of the Bible you use matter? Yes and no. For study, it is best to use a translation. Examples of translations are the King James or New King James, the NIV (New International Version) and the New Revised Standard Version. These Bibles are based on a literal translation of the Hebrew and Greek, the languages in which the original manuscripts were written.[10]

Versions of the Bible such as *The Living Bible* or *The Message* are written in modern language. That does not mean that they are not God's Word, but that they are not intended to be accurate translations from the original languages. They are meant to help people to apply the words of the Bible to their daily lives by putting the Bible's concepts into modern day language and examples.

Use the Bible of your choice as your main guide. Do not feel that other people, especially those who have studied the Bible for many years, know which Bible you should use. Choose the version or translation of the Bible that helps you understand God's Word and apply it to your life.

As you grow, you will explore other versions and translations. As you become more experienced in studying the Bible, you will find it helpful to use several translations and versions to compare as you study.

Bible reading and Bible study

Bible study must be differentiated from Bible reading. Bible reading is fast food; Bible study is nourishing spiritual food.

Bible reading as fast food

Bible study is important for understanding the meaning of what is written in the Bible. Simply reading the Bible can lead

SPIRITUAL NUTRITION

to wrong ideas about what God wants to teach us. However, reading the Bible is better than leaving our Bible sitting on the shelf. Sometimes I visited someone who attended worship regularly but did not know where his Bible was. He would eventually find a Bible on the bookshelf, blow a cloud of dust off the top (usually in my direction), and say, "This is the Bible they gave me when I graduated from fourth grade Sunday school." How can one know God's heart without knowing God's Word?

Good fast food Bible reading

Just looking at the Bible on the shelf is not adequate for our spiritual intake of God's Word any more than just looking at a bowl of almonds will put protein into our bodies. How do we open the Bible and read it in a way that is good for our daily diets when we don't have time for Bible study?

1. Use a devotional booklet such as *Our Daily Bread* or *The Secret Place* that have a Bible verse, a short meditation, and a prayer for each day. Ask your pastor or another leader in the church to help you find such a devotional magazine or booklet. Use the daily devotional in the way that fits your life, either in the morning, on your commute, before you begin your day, or in the evening. (Experiment to find your best time.) If you have time, read the Bible verse for the day from your Bible, paying attention to the verses around it and who is speaking.
2. Use one of *The One Year Bible* books each day. These books are provided in various translations and versions. For each day there is an Old Testament section, a psalm, and a New Testament section arranged so that if you read each day's verses you will read through the whole Bible in a year. Again, use the readings each day as fits your schedule. I

BIBLE STUDY: SPIRITUAL PROTEIN

use one of these books in the morning and read only one section or even part of a section. (Therefore, it takes me longer than a year to reach the end.)
3. Read a Bible passage before you go to bed.
4. Read a Bible passage before you begin your daily prayer time.
5. Listen to the Bible on CD in your car or at home. Download a Bible book onto your MP3 player and listen on your commute, while you wait in line or for an appointment, while you exercise, or while you make a meal. MP3 players can be purchased with the Bible downloaded on them. You may be able to find a podcast with a daily Bible reading.

SOMETHING FUN YOUR CHURCH CAN DO

An idea for a church to encourage Bible reading is something we did at a church in Indiana. The deacons decided to hold a Bible reading contest, called the "Bible Blast" (since the celebration would be on the 4th of July). Each person in the church was placed on a team and recorded the number of pages of the Bible that he or she read every day. Anyone who heard the passage read could count each page that was read (including anyone who could not yet read). People got their dusty Bibles off the shelf and read. Businessmen read the Bible on trips. Students read the Bible at lunch. Parents read to children, children read to parents. Families gathered together to read the Bible to each other. And all found that reading the Bible together was enjoyable and strengthened their families.

Nourishing Bible study

God's Word as food

The psalms refer to God's Word as food, more particularly honey. The words of the Lord "are sweeter than honey, than honey from the comb" (Psalm 19:10). Psalm 119, which describes the delights of God's Word, says that God's words are sweet to the taste, "sweeter than honey to my mouth" (Psalm 119:103). I like to substitute the word "chocolate" for honey. I desire God's Word more than I desire chocolate (and that's saying quite a bit!).

Bible study helps us understand God's Word. When we study the Bible we, in a sense, eat God's Word. We take in God's Word as we do our food. By feeding on God's Word we grow in Jesus.

How do I study the Bible?

Does a person need to go to seminary or learn Greek and Hebrew to understand God's Word? No. Bible study as nourishing spiritual food is not about academic study. However, certain tools will help you in your study.

NOTEBOOK. Record the passages you study and your ideas and questions. Be sure to include your insights about how what you learn applies to your life.

STUDY BIBLE. A study Bible is a Bible that has a column on the side of each page or in the middle of the page with lots of numbers. (Maybe you always wondered what those numbers were!) There is usually a bold number, which is the verse on the page, and listed under the number are references to other passages in the Bible. (Different study Bibles will use different formats.) These references can lead you to the origin of the verse or to a similar verse (or even leave you scratching your head and asking, "What does this have to do with the verse?").

BIBLE STUDY: SPIRITUAL PROTEIN

BIBLE CONCORDANCE. In a concordance ("an index of words") you can look up a word that is used in the Bible and find where the same word is used in other places in the Bible. Although many Bibles have a limited concordance in the back, a "comprehensive" concordance—a complete book with every word (except, of course, for common words like "a" and "the")—is best for Bible study. Using a concordance can help you understand the meaning of a word. A concordance is also useful for finding names of people or places in the Bible so that you can find out more about them. Your concordance can also help you find a Bible verse that you remember but can't find (if you can remember a key word).

Concordances are available for any translation of the Bible.

BIBLE DICTIONARY. In a Bible dictionary you can look up the meaning of words or learn more about a book of the Bible, a person, or a place.

BIBLE ATLAS. You can look up cities and towns mentioned in the Bible, trace the routes of the Israelites or the apostle Paul, and find out about the geography of Egypt, Israel, and Asia.

While many Bibles have one or more of these tools, separate books will give you more complete tools. You can also purchase CDs with these tools. However, these CDs can be expensive and will often have more tools that you will ever need to use.

Be wary of using internet resources. Anyone can give a definition of anything. If you find something on the internet, check it out in your reference tools.

Ask the question: What is the context of the passage?

When studying a passage of the Bible, it is crucial to look at more than one or two verses. As God's Word implies, even Satan can use the Scripture to prove what he wants to prove. (See Matthew 3:5–7.) It is important to understand the book the verses are from. Is it a psalm, history, a part of the Jewish law, a gospel, or a letter? (Use your Bible dictionary or summary at the beginning of the book in your Bible to find out the answer.)

Read before and after the verse or section you are studying to answer the questions: Who is speaking? Where does the action take place? Who is the audience? Who else is present? What else is happening? What happened or what was said just before this passage? What happens right after this passage?

Can I study the Bible by myself?

Yes. However, it is crucial to share your insights with at least one other person, preferably in a group Bible study. Why? It is easy to go off on the wrong path. (Remember the giant spiders?) Other people will help you to see where you have made a right or wrong conclusion. They will ask you questions to help you in your study. Other people can help answer or explore questions you have about the passage. (Don't be afraid to ask any question. Chances are someone else has the same question.) Keep a record of your questions in your notebook as you study.

It is important that whether you study the Bible alone or in a group, the materials you use and the group leader help you apply what you learn about God's Word to your life. Insist upon it.

What passages should I study?

There are many Bible study guides available for you to use. These guides are usually helps to study a Bible book or what the Bible says on a topic (such as love or managing one's finances). Most well known speakers and authors like Chuck Swindoll or Kay Arthur have guides for studying Bible books, people in the Bible, or subjects. Ask your pastor or a local Christian bookstore for suggestions. You can also study passages without a study guide. Choose a book of the Bible or a short section of Scripture (such as the verses used at the headings of the chapters in this book). Be sure to ask the context questions and use your study tools.

Some pastors tell the congregation what Scriptures the sermon will be based on for the next week or month. You can study those Scriptures and be a part of groups that meet to discuss them (or even start your own group.) Your study will make the sermon much more interesting for you.

How long should I study at one time?

You should probably try to study for at least a half hour at a time.

You may only be able to study the Bible this way several days a week. Don't kill yourself trying to fit in a half-hour Bible study every day if you have a family, work, and volunteer responsibilities. A friend with a full-time job and two little boys announced that she was going to get up a 5:00 A.M. every morning for Bible study. I thought, *That won't last too long!*

Try to fit in some time for study during the week. Try Bible study on the evening before your weekly worship service or on a designated evening or morning. When you find a time that works for you, write your Bible study time as an appointment on your calendar every week.

What about memorizing Bible passages?

If it works for you, do it!

Some people insist that Scripture must be memorized. I have seen memorization of Bible passages called a spiritual discipline. While I do not feel that people who have trouble with memorization should torture themselves, it is true that memorizing passages of Scripture such as Psalm 23 or Psalm 27:1 gives us something to hold onto in times of stress or fear. I am always surprised by how much Scripture I remember when I am inside the MRI chamber.

SPIRITUAL NUTRITION

An example from Elijah

As an example, we will look at 1 Kings 17:7–16.

Before you begin to study any passage of the Bible, pray that God will illuminate the Word to you. A friend of mine says that if we ask, the Holy Spirit will breathe over the text to show us what we need to understand. Sometimes I read a passage that I have read many times before and find something new in it (and I am sure that someone added the new part when I wasn't looking!).

Without application to our lives, Bible study is only an intellectual activity. God's Word is meant to apply to our lives in the world and in the church, as we interact with others and with the world's temptations. Pray that God will help you understand new insights from your study and apply them to your life.

Introduction. In 1 Kings 17, we first meet the great prophet Elijah. We learn in verse 1 that Elijah was from Tishbe in Gilead. For the curious, look up Tishbe, Gilead, and Elijah in a Bible dictionary to find out about Elijah's origins. Most Bible dictionaries will also have entries for each Bible book, so you can look up 1 Kings to find out about the whole book. Or your Bible may have a section before each book that will give you an introduction to the book. First Kings is one of the Jewish books of history, the history of the kings in Israel.

Context. In 1 Kings 17:1, Elijah is speaking to Ahab. In 1 Kings 16:29–33, we find out that Ahab is a King in Judah, married to Jezebel. Ahab "did more to provoke the Lord to anger than did all the kings of Israel before him" (v. 33). Elijah tells Ahab that there will be a drought for several years. God then tells Elijah to hide because Jezebel is going to try to have Elijah killed. While Elijah is in hiding near a brook, God sends ravens to bring bread and meat to Elijah.

After awhile, the brook dries up because of the drought (1 Kings 17:7). In verse 8, God tells Elijah to go to Zarephath of

BIBLE STUDY: SPIRITUAL PROTEIN

Sidon to a widow who will give him food. Looking in a Bible atlas, we see that Sidon is on the coast of the Mediterranean Sea in Phoenicia. A Bible dictionary tells us that Phoenicia is not part of Israel and its people believe in Baal, the Canaanite god. This woman was not a believer in God—in 1 Kings 17:12, she tells Elijah, "As surely as the Lord your God lives." Elijah's God is not her God. God has sent Elijah outside of Israel to ask for food from a non-Jewish woman.

This widow is poor and has no one to care for her and her son. She has hardly anything to eat, only enough flour and oil for one more cake of bread. Elijah asks her for a piece of bread. The definition of "bread" in my Bible dictionary says that bread was made with ground grain, water, salt, and "old dough" saved from another bread baking day. But the widow has only flour and oil. So when she says, "I don't have any bread," she means it.

Elijah promises her that if she uses what she has to make the bread for him "the jar of flour will not be used up and the jug of oil will not run dry" as long as the drought continues (17:14). She uses her "handful of flour" and "a little oil" to make a "small cake of bread," probably more like a cracker, for Elijah.

"So there was food every day" for Elijah, the woman, and her family as Elijah had promised her (17:15). Because she gave the last of her food to Elijah, she had food during the entire time of the drought.

What application to our lives can we find from this passage?

- I think about giving to those who have little by giving to the food bank, giving to Habitat for Humanity, or volunteering time to deliver or serve meals. Even if I feel that my budget is tight, I have enough to share with others. God asks me to share with those who have less.

SPIRITUAL NUTRITION

- God is going to take care of my needs. God told Elijah to stay beside a brook where he would have water and that ravens would bring food to Elijah (17:4). God had commanded the Canaanite woman to give Elijah food (17:9).
- Obedience to God. When God asks me to do something, I need to do it and not argue about it. What God promises, God will do. God promised Elijah that he would meet a Canaanite widow who would give him food. He did. God promised the widow, through Elijah, that if she did as Elijah asked, she would have flour and oil until the drought was over. She did.

What application to your own life does God speak from this passage to your heart?

In the same way that protein is an essential nutrient in our diets, Bible study is an essential spiritual nutrient. Protein is necessary for the growth of our bodies. When our bodies are injured, we require additional protein in our diets for healing.[11] In the same way, if we do not study God's Word, we will not grow and we are wide open to temptation, spiritual warfare, discouragement, and wandering off God's path.

When we study the Bible, we maintain our connection with God through God's Word. God speaks through the breath of the Holy Spirit who makes the Word alive and active in our hearts as we live each day (Hebrews 4:12).

BIBLE STUDY: SPIRITUAL PROTEIN

How much protein is in your spiritual diet?

If you are home, go find a Bible (or find one when you get home).

How long did it take you to find it? _____

Is your Bible a translation or a version? _____

Which one (e.g. NIV, King James)? _____

Is your Bible a study Bible? _____

Do you take your Bible to worship services so that you can follow the Scripture passages used in the sermon and Bible readings? _____

How often did you read the Bible in the last two weeks? _____

Where were you, what did you read, and what did you do while you read?

Did you study a Bible passage in the last two weeks? _____

Which passage did you study?

Who do you share the insights from your Bible study with? A Bible study group? Another Christian?

How often do you meet?

If you are in a Bible study group, who is in your group?

SPIRITUAL NUTRITION

Are you satisfied with this group and how the Bible is studied?

What do you like best about the group?

What would you like to change? Can you bring up these ideas for changes with your group or with the group leader?

If you are not part of a Bible study group what person could you ask to study the Bible with you?

Is there a Bible study you could start attending? Where is it and when does it meet? If you don't know of one, who could you ask?

What is the group Bible study that you remember the most?
_____

Was it a good experience? Why?

If it was a good experience, can you apply the way you studied the Bible to your study of the Bible now? How?

BIBLE STUDY: SPIRITUAL PROTEIN

Is your Bible a study Bible?_____ Do you use the references?_____

Without looking, what tools does your Bible contain besides the Scriptures?
_____
_____

Do you use these tools?

Look in your Bible and write down the study tools you find.

Do you own a

    Bible atlas _____

    Bible dictionary _____

    Comprehensive concordance to the Bible you use _____

    Do you know where they are?

    When was the last time you used each one? _____

    Do you use a notebook to record what you study and your questions and insights?

    Put these resources together to make your times of Bible study easier.

CHRISTIAN FELLOWSHIP: CARBOHYDRATES FOR SPIRITUAL ENERGY

Chapter 7

> In Christ we who are many form one body, and each member belongs to all the others.
> —Romans 12:5

Our spirits' need for Christian fellowship

When I worked in a college bookstore, it seemed as if I were the only Christian. One day my spiritual antennae started twitching when I heard another cashier talking about "her church." Yay! Another Christian! As soon as I could I asked her, "What church do you go to?" We often talked about spiritual things when we worked together. When she was diagnosed with cancer, I purchased a religious card for the other employees to sign. When I took it to her home I felt comfortable praying with her and her family.

CHRISTIAN FELLOWSHIP: CARBOHYDRATES FOR SPIRITUAL ENERGY

Our bodies' need for carbohydrates

- The chief source of energy for our bodies is carbohydrates. Eating an adequate amount of carbohydrates ensures that our bodies will not have to use the protein in our muscles for energy.
- Carbohydrates come in three forms: simple, complex, and dietary fiber.
- Simple carbohydrates are simple molecules. Therefore, the body can use simple carbohydrates quickly for energy. However, this energy surge is short and is followed by an energy drop.
- Simple carbohydrates are found in sugar, including white and brown sugar, honey, candy, soda, and syrup. Simple sugars that include vitamins and minerals are found in milk, fruits, and vegetables.
- Complex carbohydrates or starches are longer sugar molecules. Because the molecules are more complex, it takes the body time to break down starch molecules. Therefore, the energy provided by complex carbohydrates lasts over a longer period of time.
- Complex carbohydrates are found in bread, breakfast cereals, oatmeal, tortillas, popcorn, rice, and pasta. See *mypyramid.gov* "Inside the pyramid," "Grains," and the right hand tab: "Tips to help you eat whole grains" for a discussion of whole grains and refined grains.
- Dietary fiber is essential in our diets. Because a discussion of dietary fiber is not needed here, a good reference is *Nutrition for Dummies*, pp. 105–112.

SPIRITUAL NUTRITION

Carbohydrates and fast foods

- Fast foods, including soda, candy, and most cookies and chips, contain "empty calories," calories that have little nutritional value for our bodies.
- Good choices when eating fast food are apple slices, 2 percent milk as a beverage, salads (without too much cheese or the taco shell bowl), and carrot sticks. Fried potato products, such as French fries or potato chips, have too much fat to be considered a good source of carbohydrates. The fried fruit pie—forget it!

Just as carbohydrates give us energy for living our daily lives, meeting other Christians when we are out in the world gives us energy. We know that we are in contact with someone who understands and shares our grounding in Jesus Christ. Because we are connected in Jesus we can ask other Christians to pray for us and know that they understand and will pray for us. They become our spiritual allies in the places that we work, study, play, and spend our time.

Our physical bodies need a continuous supply of energy to function properly and our spirits need a continuous supply of spiritual energy to serve Jesus in the world. Our source of spiritual energy is Jesus Christ. An important way that we connect to Jesus comes from our connection with other Christians.

What is Christian fellowship?

One of the members of my youth group defined "Christian fellowship" as "a bunch of fellows on a ship." While he meant it to be a silly answer, it is a good definition. We are all on this "ship"—this earth, this community, this workplace, this

CHRISTIAN FELLOWSHIP: CARBOHYDRATES FOR SPIRITUAL ENERGY

church. Christian fellowship is the Holy Spirit joining together those who believe in Jesus Christ.

Can't I just be a believer in Jesus on my own?

Nope. A follower of Jesus Christ is a part of a body, the body of Christ, the church. The statement, "I can be a Christian without the church" is nonsensical. To be a Christian is to be part of the church, the body of Christ.

What if your arm decided it was tired of being attached to your body and detached itself to go on its own way? Soon the severed arm would begin to rot, putrefy, and die. One Sunday, I had very graphically described the stinking, maggoty arm as a sermon illustration. A woman approached me after the service. She did not attend worship very often because her husband refused to let her come and she had to sneak out. She said, almost in tears, "I don't want to become a dead arm!" No follower of Jesus Christ exists independently of other believers.

Those who believe in Jesus Christ are joined together by the Holy Spirit. In the Gospel of John, chapter 14, Jesus is speaking to his followers about the Holy Spirit. Jesus says to them, using the plural form of "you," "If you love me, you will obey what I command. And I will ask the Father, and he will give you another Counselor to be with you forever—the Spirit of truth. The world cannot accept him, because it neither sees him nor knows him. But you know him, for he lives with you and will be in you" (John 14:15–17). The Holy Spirit lives in us, connecting us with other believers and together, to Jesus.

Even though a believer may at times experience physical isolation from other believers (perhaps by illness or imprisonment), he or she is still a part of the church.[12]

Jesus speaks of our need for each other in his description of himself as the "true vine" in John 15:1. Jesus says, "I am the vine; you are the branches. . . . [A]part from me you can do nothing" (John 15:5). The church, the union of the followers of Jesus Christ, is "in Christ." Our power to live for Jesus is given by Jesus himself if we stay connected to him in the same way that a leaf receives nourishment when it is connected to the vine. When we are connected to Jesus we are connected to one another—the rest of the branches and leaves on the vine—sharing light, life, and love.

In the apostle Paul's books in the New Testament he uses the pronoun that is translated "one another" forty-one times. Believers in Jesus are to look out, not for their own interests, but for one another's interests. Paul uses the metaphor of the body of Christ to describe his vision of the church as a whole with each believer and each local church playing a necessary part: "In Christ we who are many form one body, and each member belongs to all the others" (Romans 12:5).

In 1 Corinthians 12:12–27, Paul expands this metaphor of the church as a body. The body is made up of many parts (v. 14) that are equally important. Each part needs all the other parts. "Its parts should have equal concern for each other" (v. 25) so that "if one part suffers, every part suffers with it; if one part is honored, every part rejoices with it" (v. 26). Each believer is an important and necessary part of the church (v. 27). Believers need each other.

Good fast food Christian fellowship

For the best spiritual nutrition, we need to spend time with other believers in Bible study, prayer, or talking together. But our busy schedules do not always permit us to spend enough time with each other.

We can encourage each other often, if not every day. We can send our Christian family members and friends a quick e-mail, text message, or card. We can put the name of a Christian friend on each day of a calendar. If we both have e-mail, we can send a short message telling our friend that we will be praying

CHRISTIAN FELLOWSHIP: CARBOHYDRATES FOR SPIRITUAL ENERGY

for him or her that day. I feel strength when I receive a message from a friend who has been praying for me.

Christian fellowship that nourishes us

To keep our connection with Jesus strong we need to spend time with other believers. Our lives are full of small and huge traumas and discouragements. We feel like our children hate us, our boss is a control freak, we get bad news from the doctor. The joys in our lives become more special when shared. Our relationship with other Christians helps us to give and receive courage and support from each other through our common bond in Jesus.

Being with other Christians in Bible studies, book groups, prayer groups, retreats, or a day spent in recreation gives us good spiritual nutrition. Even small amounts of time spent with other Christians over a meal, coffee, or on the phone can give us quality spiritual nourishment.

Biblical examples of nourishing fellowship

In both the Old Testament and the New Testament we see how the encouragement given by others gives us the energy to go on.

An Old Testament tale: encouragement

In the history of Israel, the time of the judges was a time when "everyone did as he saw fit." There was internal strife within the nation of Israel. In Judges 19, the men of the tribe of Benjamin who were living in Gibeah killed the concubine of a priest. (That priests had mistresses tells us something of the times). The priest cut her body in twelve pieces and sent them to "all parts of Israel." Then the men of Israel met and declared war on Gibeah. (War was declared often in those days.)

SPIRITUAL NUTRITION

In Judges 20:21, we read that during this war, Benjamites killed 22,000 Israelites on the first day of fighting. 22,000 deaths is a cause for discouragement. But the next verse tells us that "the men of Israel encouraged one another" and reformed their ranks instead of giving up and running away.

The encouragement of their fellow soldiers helped each soldier to stand firm in the face of desperate odds. In the same way, the encouragement of other believers helps us hold each other up and helps us to keep on going and not give up even in the face of defeat and discouragement. (The men of Israel, with God's help, ultimately defeated the men of the tribe of Benjamin. For an exciting story, read the rest of Judges 20.)

From the New Testament book of Hebrews

In the book of Hebrews we get a glimpse of how important it is for us to encourage each other so that we are spiritually healthy enough to ward off the sickness caused by wrong actions.

Hebrews 3:12 warns us that a sinful heart turns away from God. We are admonished to "encourage one another daily, as long as it is called Today, so that none of you may be hardened by sin's deceitfulness. We have come to share in Christ if we hold firmly till the end the confidence we had at first" (Hebrews 3:13–14). The encouragement of other believers keeps us from turning away from God to sin. Sin is "deceitful," promising that we will receive our heart's desire if we turn from God. A seventeenth century spiritual work, *Precious Remedies Against Satan's Devices* by Puritan Thomas Brooks, describes the lure of sin as "golden bait" concealing a hook that Satan will use to draw us away from God. Other believers help us recognize sin in our lives and help us stand against it, just as the Israelites

CHRISTIAN FELLOWSHIP: CARBOHYDRATES FOR SPIRITUAL ENERGY

stood against the Benjamites. How long would one soldier alone have had the courage to stand in the face of such terrible odds?

In a case of adultery that shocked many people in one church, the participants said, "God wants us to be happy." Interestingly, both parties had stopped coming to worship services and other activities of the church although they had once been quite active. We need each other to help us to stand against the lies of sin.

Spiritual statins

Christian fellowship could be called a spiritual statin. Statins are drugs that help prevent the buildup of plaque in our arteries that could lead to a heart attack or stroke. When the arteries of our physical hearts become "hardened" by plaque, blood cannot easily flow through our arteries. Sin hardens our spiritual arteries. Spiritual arteries that are hardened by sin impede the flow of the Holy Spirit through our spiritual lives. The encouragement of other believers can help prevent the hardening of our spirits that could lead to spiritual death. The encouragement of other Christians leads to and helps us maintain spiritual health.

The notes in my study Bible for these verses from Hebrews 3 lead me to Hebrews 10:24–25: "And let us consider how we may spur one another on toward love and good deeds. Let us not give up meeting together, as some are in the habit of doing, but let us encourage one another—and all the more as you see the Day approaching." When Christians join together we not only encourage one another to stand firm in Jesus against the deceit of sin but we also "spur one another on" to do good and loving acts. Without the fellowship of other Christians we will be seduced down wrong paths and give in to discouragement, falling away from the faith. We will cry, "Why has God done this to me?" and turn away. When we are in need, other believers can walk with us and hold us up until we are able to walk again.

Eating the right spiritual carbohydrates: gossip and tearing down

In the same way that we must watch the intake of simple sugars in our diets, the fellowship of other Christians must be carefully monitored in our spiritual diets. The energy rush provided by foods with empty calories is like spending time with others who gossip. It is exciting to be the first one to dish the dirt on someone else. That chocolate bar tastes a lot better than a bowl of oat bran. But gossip is harmful to the individual Christian and to the whole body of Christ, tearing down instead of building up. As the apostle Paul reminds us, "Do not let any unwholesome talk come out of your mouths, but only what is helpful for building others up according to their needs, that it may benefit those who listen." Such "unwholesome talk" grieves the Holy Spirit (Ephesians 4:29–30).

Do we spend time with whiny believers who gripe about everything? Do we spend time with those who gossip or with those who incite divisions in the church? When we talk with our Christian friends, do we talk about how we can pray for one another or about how inadequate our pastor is? What we talk about with our Christian friends can help us know whether our relationship with other Christians is promoting our spiritual health or giving us a diet that will eventually lead to a diseased spirit. If we are serious about maintaining spiritual health, we must be ruthless and vigilant in avoiding and stopping talk that discourages or tears down. We must have the courage to ask God to reveal to us whether our Christian fellowship is encouraging and healthy or making us weak and sick. We must listen to and act on God's answer.

CHRISTIAN FELLOWSHIP: CARBOHYDRATES FOR SPIRITUAL ENERGY

Can I take in too much Christian fellowship?

Absolutely. Some people have very few, if any, friends outside of the church or other Christian groups. Too much Christian fellowship leads to the same result as eating more carbohydrates than are needed for the body's energy—excess fat.[13] Some Christians need a low carbohydrate diet of each other—they spend too much time with other Christians. We are not called to hide together behind our church walls. Jesus calls us to go out into the world to make disciples (Matthew 28:18) and to serve (Matthew 25:31–45).

On the first day we moved into an apartment after living in the college dorm, my roommate and I decided to make chocolate chip cookie dough—just to eat the dough. All of the dough in one sitting. The next day I had a sugar hangover. Spending time only in the presence of other believers is like eating a diet of just cookie dough. Cookie dough has some protein in the ingredients (flour, eggs, nuts) and even some vitamins. However, the constant energy spike from the simple sugars in the cookie dough will eventually lead to a sick body if we live on cookie dough alone (even chocolate chip cookie dough). This admonition includes pastors. Encourage your pastor to have a life outside of the church even though it will mean less time to be preoccupied with you and other church members. Even pastors need to be out in the world as Jesus commanded.

What if I don't get enough spiritual carbohydrates?

Our bodies need carbohydrates in our diets. If carbohydrate intake is inadequate, the body will begin to break down protein (our muscles) for the energy it needs. When the protein is gone the body will die. In our spiritual lives, the loss of spiritual energy and the breakdown of spiritual health occur when we try to live our lives outside of Christian fellowship by trying to be Christians by ourselves.

The lack of spiritual energy can have effects on our physical health. I worked in a public defender's office where our caseload included many driving under the influence cases. These cases were repetitive and draining. Attorneys and support staff de-stressed after work at a local bar. While I am not opposed to drinking, I was concerned about using alcohol to relieve my stress so I did not participate in the nightly ritual. As far as I knew, none of my co-workers were Christians. I felt isolated from the other employees. I experienced physical and spiritual burnout. After having gall bladder surgery, I was not able to recover my physical or emotional strength and was eventually laid off.

Christians need one another both to thrive and to survive in the world.

Jesus calls us to go out into the world (Matthew 28:19). To be the people Jesus calls us to be in the world, we need to take in carbohydrates for spiritual energy—the support of other Christians with whom we are joined by the Holy Spirit.

Our interactions with other Christians need to be like whole grains—talk and actions that build up instead of tear down. We need other believers to pray for us and support us even as we support and encourage them.

CHRISTIAN FELLOWSHIP: CARBOHYDRATES FOR SPIRITUAL ENERGY

Testing your spiritual energy level

How much time do you spend at your local church or with your Christian friends? Out in the world?

What groups or activities do you participate in outside of your church? Name them.

How many Christians are in these groups? Name them.

How do you support those Christians you have named?
If you work outside the home, what Christians can you name in your workplace? If you are a student, how many Christians are in your classes or live in your dorm. Name them.

How do you know they are Christians?

How do you support those Christians you have named?

Do they know you are a Christian? How?

How do you connect with other Christians?

    At church

SPIRITUAL NUTRITION

    At school or work

    Other places

Do you spend time in Bible study or prayer with other Christians?

    When was the last time you did so?
    What did you talk about?

Name three of your closest Christian friends.

    How often do you talk together?

    What do you talk about?

    How do you support each other as believers?

What things could you do to keep from gossip when you are with your Christian friends?

WORSHIP: HEALTHY FATS FOR A HEALTHY HEART

CHAPTER 8

> Worship is at the very center of all Christian living.
>
> —N.T. Wright[14]

Our spirits' need for healthy fats

At 11:00 a.m. on a warm spring Sunday morning, the worship service in the little town's church was about to begin. As people settled themselves in the pews I prayed silently, "Lord, send your Holy Spirit in power on this place and these people." Immediately there was a loud WHUMP from the back of the room. My first thought was, "Does the Holy Spirit WHUMP?" and then that there had been a car crash outside the building. People in the back got up. I thought, *Why are you getting up?* It was only an accident.

No one had stood up. Those in the back pews had been pushed up by the impact of a farm truck that had hit the side of the church building. When we all went outside, we could see

WORSHIP: HEALTHY FATS FOR A HEALTHY HEART

the brush guard of the big, black pickup resting on the support beam between the belfry/entrance and the sanctuary. Shaken at the realization that a few inches to the right would have meant a pickup in the sanctuary and serious injuries from flying daggers of stained glass, people wandered in a daze outside the building.

What do I do? They never taught us in seminary what to do when a truck runs into the church building right before the service starts. I did the only thing to do. Worship. Gather everyone into the fellowship hall. Pray to center our hearts, sing "Amazing Grace," give a five-minute sermon sound bite on grace, pray a blessing, and send everyone home.

Our bodies' need for healthy fats

- Healthy fats are necessary in our diets.
- Healthy fats are carriers for the fat-soluble vitamins A, D, E, and K, which help our bodies maintain healthy bones and tissues.[15]
- Healthy fats provide our bodies with essential fatty acids. (Our bodies need them but cannot make them.)[16]
- Healthy fats help keep our hair and skin from being dry and scaly.
- Fats, along with carbohydrates and proteins, are sources of energy for our bodies.

What are healthy fats?

Healthy fats, which MyPyramid calls "oils," are fats that are liquid at room temperature. These fats are unsaturated fats: monounsaturated fats and polyunsaturated fats. Omega-3 fatty acids are polyunsaturated fats that may help prevent heart disease by lowering LDLs (low-density lipoproteins popularly

SPIRITUAL NUTRITION

known as "bad cholesterol") and maintaining or raising HDLs (high-density lipoproteins or "good cholesterol").[17] Healthy fats can help keep plaque from forming in our blood vessels. When plaque breaks off of the deposits in our blood vessels, a heart attack or stroke can result.

- The key to eating healthy fats is moderation.
- Plant-based oils like olive oil and canola oil are healthy fats.
- Other foods with healthy fats are avocados, walnuts, and almonds.
- Omega-3 fatty acids are found in salmon, flaxseeds, flax oil, and walnuts.[18]
- Choose low-fat or non-fat milk and milk products.

What is unhealthy fat?

Unhealthy fat is fat that is hard at room temperature. These fats are saturated fat and trans fats. Trans fats are created when hydrogen atoms are added to fats or oils (a process known as "hydrogenation"). The solid fats that result from hydrogenation give commercial baked products a long shelf life while keeping their flavor. However, the hydrogenated or partially hydrogenated oils that are created—trans fats—are unhealthy fats.[19]

- Unhealthy fat is the fat that you can see on food: the white fat on beef, pork, or poultry, including the skin.
- Solid fats, such as butter, stick margarine, and Crisco shortening also contain unhealthy fats.
- Tropical oils such as palm kernel and coconut oil are high in saturated fats.[20]
- Foods with unhealthy fats taste good but have many calories.

WORSHIP: HEALTHY FATS FOR A HEALTHY HEART

- Unhealthy fat is sneaky. It is found in many great-tasting commercial baked goods such as chips, cookies, and crackers.
- We must learn to read packaging labels and avoid food containing trans-fat, hydrogenated and partially-hydrogenated oils of any kind.

Fats and fast food

If you have read this far, you don't need me to explain it. What makes a Krispy Kreme doughnut taste so good? KFC extra-crispy chicken? Pizza Hut cheese-stuffed-crust pizza? Big Macs? Whoppers? French fries?

Unhealthy fats such as the oil for deep frying are used to cook fast foods because they are cheap and can be reused many times. We create our own poor health by demanding the tastiness of fast food that comes from the unhealthy fat in hamburgers, whole milk cheese, and chicken skin and the fats in which our food is fried.

Worship is to our spiritual health what healthy fats are to our physical health. Worship grounds us in God and helps us to have healthy hearts.

What is worship?

Some people say, "I can worship God anywhere." This statement is true. Worship, the adoration of God, is an attitude. When we worship God, we lift the eyes of our spirits beyond our daily problems and worries. We are reminded that God is in charge of our lives and walks with us each day and each hour. Worship is an attitude of coming to God, either alone

SPIRITUAL NUTRITION

or with others, with all that we have. We bring before God our families, our work, our sickness, and our joys—all that we are—and offer these to God in praise. Some days we have a lot to offer; some days we feel that we have little. What we have we bring into God's presence.

In this chapter we are focusing on corporate worship—worship with others. Do we need a church building to worship God? Hopefully, we are showing our reverence for God in all that we do and wherever we go. But we are called to come together at an appointed place, on an appointed day to give our praise to God in the presence of others who also come to worship God.[21]

Worship: coming together to say, together, "Our God is worthy to be praised." Worship as an essential spiritual nutrient must include corporate worship. There is a discipline to dragging ourselves out of bed, getting dressed, and going out to worship with others. Sometimes someone will tell me, "I just didn't feel like coming to church today." To which I reply, "That is the time you need to come to worship the most." Worship with others helps us lift our eyes to God and away from ourselves.

Worship is not about waiting for someone else to "feed" us or give us something that makes it worth our while to sit in a sanctuary for a worship service. We bring ourselves to worship, expecting God's presence and God's touch as we bring our praise and celebrate the wonder of God.

How is worship with others like healthy fats in our diets?

In the same way that healthy fats can help keep the arteries in our hearts from the buildup of heart-attack and stroke-inducing plaque, when we come to God in corporate worship we create health in our spiritual hearts. Coming to worship just to see our friends or because we think we are earning Brownie points from God is like eating unhealthy fats. Worship becomes something we do for us. Healthy-fat worship is about God and for God, not about us. Praising God keeps our hearts from becoming hardened by sin, giving in to our desires to get what we want, and the enticements of the devil. We remember whose we are and the goodness of the One who keeps us in his love.

A heart-healthy Old Testament worship service

Nehemiah 8:1–12 is a model of worship that we will do well to consider carefully. In this act of worship the Israelites show us all the elements necessary for heart-healthy corporate worship—adoring and praising God together.

1. In verse 1, the people gathered together. They told Ezra the scribe to bring out the book of the Law of Moses. This book was probably all or part of the first five books in our Bible—Genesis, Exodus, Leviticus, Numbers, and Deuteronomy.[22]

    The people were hungry to hear the words of the book of the Law.

    In the same way we gather together in a place of worship. We greet each other and share the latest news. There is a musical prelude during which we ready ourselves to praise God (not just keep visiting). We then call each other to worship and ask God to be present with us as we worship. We sing a hymn of praise to prepare our hearts to worship.

    All this, the gathering, is because our hearts are hungry to hear the Word of God. Our hearts are hungry to hear, once again, the story of Jesus Christ: his life, death, and resurrection—the destruction of the power of sin and death over our lives. We hunger to hear the Word. We feel that our lives are out of shape, pulled apart by the events of the

SPIRITUAL NUTRITION

week. We know that it is only God's Word that can heal us and put us back into shape.

2. In verse 3 we read that all the men, women, and some children came to hear the Word: "All the people listened attentively to the Book of the Law."[23] In verse 5 the people listened to Ezra read the law from daybreak until noon, at least six hours. They stood up the whole time. No one took the opportunity to take a nap. (You know who you are!) No one took the opportunity to plan their next week's activities. All the people stood and listened. (Imagine the outcry if our pastors were to ask us to stand for even a one-hour worship service!)

   In some traditions, worshippers stand during the reading of the New Testament lesson. Standing honors God who has given us the Son, God's Word made flesh.

3. In verses 7–8 the priests (Levites) "helped the people understand the law." This was either the first Sunday school or a series of sermons: "They read from the book, making it clear and giving the meaning, so that the people could understand what was being read."

   Now there is an idea! Someone used to criticize my sermons because people could understand them. (Instead of using big theological words, I shared the meaning of the words.) I say, the Word is just words unless people can understand it. Understanding is the purpose of illustrations in a sermon. Illustrations bring the Word to life.

   The Word transfixed the people of Israel. They heard the history of their deliverance from Egypt, the great deeds of Moses, and the leading of the people into the Promised Land. The interpretation of the Word brought great rejoicing. The people had a big party "because they now understood the words that had been made known to them" (Nehemiah 8:12). The purpose of preaching is to help to

WORSHIP: HEALTHY FATS FOR A HEALTHY HEART

make the Word real—real and applicable in the lives of those who hear.

The people gathered together. They heard the Word and were helped to understand it.

4. The people prayed. In the presence of God and each other they confessed their great sin.

Before reading the Word, Ezra praised the Lord (8:6). "And all the people answered, 'Amen, Amen,' lifting up their hands."

In the psalms, the lifting up of hands signifies prayer. A worshipper lifts up her hands in supplication (request) (Psalm 28:2 and Lamentations 2:19) or in praise (Psalm 63:4; 134:2). In worship we lift our hands toward heaven, asking God to come and be with us. The people in Nehemiah 8 lifted up their hands. "Then they bowed down and worshiped the Lord with their faces to the ground" (v. 6).

The people were overwhelmed by the love of God. These men and women had just returned from years of exile in a foreign country. God had sent them into exile because they had refused to worship God alone and continued to worship the gods of wood and stone that the nations around them worshiped. These people had exile fresh in their hearts. They knew just how much love God showed to them when God returned them to their own land when they deserved to die in exile.

Prayer is a vital part of worship.

5. The people responded to the Word with tears. "Nehemiah the governor, Ezra the priest and scribe, and the Levites who were instructing the people said to them all, 'This day is sacred to the Lord your God. Do not mourn or weep.' For all the people had been weeping as they listened to the words of the Law" (v. 9).

The gathering, the prayer, the hearing of the Word—the worship of the people of God—was not an occasion for weeping but an occasion for joy. Nehemiah told the people, "The joy of the Lord is your strength" (v. 9). In our gathering together, in our hearing of the Word and our prayer, we sense that, no matter how messed up our lives seem, we are strong, not in our own might or intelligence or wealth, but in the joy of the presence of the Lord in our lives. Worship with other believers draws us back to who we are as God's own people.

6. Nehemiah blessed the people in verse 10, saying: "Go and enjoy choice foods and sweet drinks, and send some to those who have nothing prepared. This day is sacred to our Lord. Do not grieve, for the joy of the Lord is your strength."

We are sent out from worship with a blessing. Someone once asked me why I did not end services with a prayer. I do. But it is a special prayer, a "benediction," a prayer asking for God to bless each one as he or she goes out into the world.

Giving

During a worship service we often have the opportunity to give. When we give monetary gifts, we are reminded that none of what we have is the result of our own hard work and ingenuity. All that we have is the result of the goodness of the giving God.

There are other ways to give during worship.

I had the privilege of leading high school youth at a national youth conference in learning about worship. One group prepared an outdoor evening worship service for all those who were attending the conference center. Each person coming to worship was asked to bring a rock. As the offering, each rock was placed in a basket to remind everyone that God is our

WORSHIP: HEALTHY FATS FOR A HEALTHY HEART

Rock. (Unfortunately, the size of the rock was not specified. A few people brought rocks that looked like boulders.)

On another occasion, a college-age retreat, the offering was an act of giving of ourselves. Worship was held on Sunday morning just before we left to return home. As the offering, we cleaned the building in which we were holding the retreat. One group cleaned the bathroom, one group the kitchen, one group the meeting area, one group the sleeping areas. We heard later that the manager of the facility was stunned when she came in with her cleaning supplies and found that the building was already clean.

Giving in worship is the giving of that with which God has blessed us—money, time, ourselves.

Communion

We also have the opportunity to take communion, sometimes called "The Lord's Table," together. In some traditions, communion is taken every Sunday. In some, communion is taken less often. When we worship together we are a living symbol of the body of Christ, who was raised out of death to give us life. When we come to the Lord's table and partake of the bread and wine (or juice), we remember, together, the love that God showed us in giving us his only Son to take our punishment on the cross. We remember that Jesus Christ is in our midst and that he has promised to come again to take us home.

On one Ash Wednesday (the beginning of Lent, forty days before Easter) I went to an Episcopal service. I had always had grape juice as the communion "wine." Here, they served real wine, awful wine. It was raw and bitter. At the moment I tasted the bitter wine I understood that the cross was not about Wonder Bread and sweet grape juice but about suffering and torture and death.

SPIRITUAL NUTRITION

Through taking communion together, as one body, we remember how Jesus Christ gave himself for us. We give him praise and thanks for his love and for his loving presence with us.

A favorite communion happened many years ago on the beach at the Oregon coast. Our high school youth group was ending a fun day of play with a worship service. We discovered that the only liquid we had was cola and the closest thing to bread was potato chips. I discovered on that evening that communion is not what we eat, as symbolic as bread and wine are, but about remembering and celebrating the love of Jesus within the community of believers.

INCREASE YOUR WORSHIP HEALTH IN ONE MONTH

Try these ideas for a month to help you get more from the worship services you attend:

WEEK 1: After you get home, write down or describe the service to someone who was not there (the order of the service, what was said or done).

WEEK 2: Take notes during the sermon. What was the main point the preacher tried to make?

WEEK 3: Ask the preacher a question about the sermon after the service (in person, on the phone, or by e-mail). During the sermon, you may want to write down the questions you have.

WEEK 4: Could you find a theme in the service (in the hymns, songs, Bible readings, prayers, and sermon)?

WORSHIP: HEALTHY FATS FOR A HEALTHY HEART

Sometimes we think we should eat no fats in our diet. I tried that once, when I was preparing for a bodybuilding competition. At the end of a few weeks I was ready to throw yet another dinner of dressing-free salad and dry chicken breast at the wall. We need healthy fats in our diet for our bodies to function properly—to be able to think and create and move and live.

The healthy fat in our diet and in our bodies is like worship to our spirits. Worship in which we come together and bring the best that we have to God keeps our spiritual arteries from becoming hardened by isolation and selfishness. Worship in which we come to God, expecting God's touch, gives power to our spiritual lives as we live for Jesus every day.

SPIRITUAL NUTRITION

What kind of fat is in your spiritual diet?

Define or describe what the word "worship" means to you.

Do you attend a worship service regularly?_____
How often?_____

What do you do to prepare for the service?

Do you do any special activities on the night before, such as listen to Christian music, read the Bible, or have quiet time?

What do you do on the morning before you go to the service?

If your answer is "nothing," you might try having a quiet night before your worship service. On the morning of the service, play Christian music during breakfast and in the car. If you have children, a quiet preparation time on the morning before the service can be difficult. To minimize the chaos, try some strategies the night

WORSHIP: HEALTHY FATS FOR A HEALTHY HEART

before like setting out clothes, deciding what's for breakfast and prayer.

How do you feel about the worship services you attend?

Does your attitude make a difference in how you feel after the service? (Think of a time when you were in a bad mood or had just had happy news.)

What could you do to have a better attitude about the service?

Do you ever participate as a leader in the worship service (praying, reading Scripture, participating as a part of a music team, or giving the children's message)? If you would like to, ask your pastor how you can help.

PHILIPPIANS 4:8: SPIRITUAL VITAMINS

CHAPTER 9

We take captive every thought to make it obedient to Christ.
—2 Corinthians 10:5

I will set before my eyes no vile thing.
—Psalm 101:3

Our spirits' need for thinking on good things

I confess. I like to listen to AC/DC. Of course, I only listen to the music. AD/DC's lyrics are black, speak of the pride of being "On the Highway to Hell," and are extremely sexually suggestive. (Okay, explicit.) I only listen to the music. But can my brain block out the lyrics that are streaming into it?

Sometimes what is good for our spiritual health isn't as clear as we wish it were. Sometimes we know what to do and choose to put the unhealthy thoughts in our minds anyway

PHILIPPIANS 4:8: SPIRITUAL VITAMINS

with creative rationalizations that don't fool anyone, especially ourselves.

Our bodies' need for vitamins

Vitamins are substances that our bodies need in small amounts. Our bodies need vitamins to build body tissues (bones, skin, eyes, and nerves), form red blood cells, ward off disease or infection, and promote healing. Vitamins help our bodies use the protein, carbohydrates, and healthy fats we eat to make the energy we need to live our lives. We need vitamins in our daily diets to keep us healthy.

What foods provide vitamins?

A balanced diet of vegetables, fruits, nuts, low fat or non-fat milk products, and whole and enriched grains will supply adequate vitamins in our diets. Animal products such as low-fat meats, eggs, and fish are also sources of vitamins.

Grains are often milled to make them faster to cook or to eat. Examples are white rice, white flour, quick cooking cereals, breakfast cereals in a box, and frozen dinners. A label on a package of bread or cereal that says "fortified" or "enriched" means that the B vitamins (and iron) lost in processing have been put back into the product. Although whole and enriched grains have some of the same vitamins, eating whole grains adds additional vitamins, minerals, and fiber to our diets.

Can't I just take a vitamin pill?

Unfortunately, no. A multi-vitamin is considered "insurance" against a diet that may lack enough vitamins. However,

SPIRITUAL NUTRITION

foods provide nutrition that vitamin pills do not, such as fiber, phytochemicals (found in plants), and antioxidants.

What about vitamins and fast food?

You can probably answer this question yourself. The best source of vitamins in fast foods is salads and fresh fruits or vegetables, such as carrot sticks and apple slices.

Salads should have as little fat as possible—fat-free or low-fat dressing, a minimal amount of cheese, grilled, and skinless chicken breast. Skip the croutons and the taco shell bowl. Bagged lettuce, spinach, and pre-made salads are good supermarket choices.

Vitamins help our bodies use the nutrients we eat in our food. To ensure that our prayer, Bible study, Christian fellowship, and worship will keep us spiritually healthy we need to take into our minds what builds up our spirits.

We find the list of our spiritual vitamins in Philippians 4:8: "Whatever is true, whatever is noble, whatever is right, whatever is pure, whatever is lovely, whatever is admirable—if anything is excellent or praise-worthy—think about such things."

The world hurls so much at our minds every day from the radio, television, billboards, magazines, our computers, even our cell phones. Much of what assails us has the opposite qualities of the praiseworthy things listed in Philippians 4:8. Not everything we hear or read or see is bad for us. How do we know what is bad or good? John Ortberg in his book, *God Is Closer Than You Think*, cautions that, "As our bodies are fed by food, so our spirits are fed by words with ideas and images.

PHILIPPIANS 4:8: SPIRITUAL VITAMINS

We are flooded by words that can mislead us, so we need to feed our minds each day from the Word of God."[24] Bible study helps us to recognize healthful and harmful sensory input.

Philippians 4:8

Let's look at the list of spiritual vitamins in this verse.

What is "true." We believe that Jesus is the Truth because he said so: "I am the way and the truth and the life" (John 14:6). Anything that has the characteristics of Jesus—love, kindness, and compassion, or exhibits concern for the poor and oppressed—is true. There are no hidden motives with the truth. (That may let out most advertising!) We must be like the shopkeepers in Western movies who bite the gold piece they are given to see if it is real gold. What is true is *what is real, not false.*

What is "noble" or "worthy." Things that are "noble" lift the mind. For the Greeks, this word was used for the gods—of splendid, magnificent things above the human realm. For us, the word "noble" denotes a position of honor, *something to admire or to respect.*[25] What is noble is a twenty-four-carat gold bracelet compared to a gold-colored plastic bracelet or Godiva chocolate compared to a bar of artificially flavored chocolate.

What is "right" is something that is *just and has integrity.*

What is "pure" is what is like God (1 John 3:3). For a time, products were produced that were clear—dish soap, soda, toothpaste—to show that these products were pure and, therefore, we should purchase them.

What is "lovely" is *pleasing and "calls forth love"* from the one seeing it.

What is "admirable," again, is *praiseworthy and attracts others.*

SPIRITUAL NUTRITION

These attributes refer not so much to things we read or see but to how we act. What personality traits bring forth admiration and affection from others? What kind of people do you like to be around? We are drawn to people who are honest, yet tactful; people who are kind; people who are who they claim to be. These are people who call us to be more than we think we can be, who help us to be better people.

When we take our spiritual vitamins we put into our minds:

- what is good,
- what is kind,
- what is compassionate, and
- what points us to the ways of Jesus.

Each of us must allow the Holy Spirit to open our hearts so that we can understand what is good and right for us to think about.

Richard Carlson, the author of *Don't Sweat the Small Stuff,* reminds us in his book, *Easier Than You Think,* that it is our own minds that control what we think about.[26] Have you ever known someone for whom life seemed to be a miserable sentence of purgatory? It does not matter what our circumstances are; we choose the thoughts that cause us to look at life as misery or as a joyful opportunity.

The apostle Paul says the same thing. He calls us to think about what is true and right and good. We will need to call upon the strength of God to help us change long-entrenched habits of negative thinking. Changing our thinking is possible and essential to achieving optimal spiritual health.

We are all different

Each of our bodies requires, and will require during our lives, different amounts of vitamins, depending upon our age,

PHILIPPIANS 4:8: SPIRITUAL VITAMINS

gender, level of activity, any illness or injury we have, and our stress levels. In the same way each of us will respond differently to what we hear and see. Some feel that romance novels are trash and no one should read them. Others feel the same way about Harry Potter or Captain Underpants books.

During a group Bible study one morning, someone said, "Oh, those Captain Underpants books are terrible." I asked if she had read one. "No." She thought the books were terrible because someone told her they were. It is important that we do not just accept the opinions of others. We need to understand our culture and the things our friends are seeing and reading so that we can talk with them intelligently.[27] Paul agrees. In his list in Philippians 4:8, Paul uses some words that are not used anywhere else in Scripture, words which had meaning for the Greeks to whom he was proclaiming the good news of Jesus. Paul spoke in words that those to whom he was speaking could understand.

Are romance novels, Harry Potter, or Captain Underpants *per se* terrible? The real question is how do these books affect *me*? How do they affect *you*? When something that we see, hear, or read is disturbing to us, we need to put it down or turn it off. Some things, such as child pornography, are always wrong for any believer to put into his or her mind and heart. Many things that come to our eyes, ears, and brain seem innocuous. Newspaper ads may hardly register in our minds unless we are looking for something to buy. But for some men, the department store ads in the newspaper showing bras become pornography. (See *Every Man's Battle* by Stephen Arterburn.)

The question is not, how do these things affect others? The question is, does what *you* put into *your* mind cause you to be upset or to have disturbing thoughts or do things that you know are not right for you to do?

This question is one that must be asked every day of everything that comes into our minds. I think of two examples

SPIRITUAL NUTRITION

from my own life. The new church computer had a solitaire program installed. After having played over two thousand games in about two weeks (I'll just play one more), I realized that I was becoming addicted to that program. So I deleted it (with a sigh).

On Saturday evenings I would watch *Law and Order SVU*, a television series that portrays a police sex crimes investigation unit. On the nights after I had watched the program, I would have disturbing dreams about cases I had defended when I was a lawyer. I would wake in a sweat. For me, it is best not to watch that television show. Is computer solitaire bad? Is *Law and Order SVU* bad for a disciple of Jesus to watch? I can only answer, yes, for me. For you, I don't know.

To determine if what you put in your mind is good for you, you must be very honest with yourself and listen to the Holy Spirit speaking to your heart. Then act on the leading of the Spirit without argument. If something seems wrong, turn it off or put it down.

Chocolate or dirt?

For one children's message on Sunday morning, I had two mixing bowls in front of me. In one bowl was cocoa powder. In the other was potting soil, fresh from the bag. I told the kids I was going to make them a cake. Should I use the chocolate or the dirt? Of course, there were wails of outrage that I would even think of making a cake with dirt, even though it was clean, sanitized potting soil. We talked about what it means to put dirt in our minds instead of chocolate. The youth leader told me that, as she came into the room at the start of the meeting that same night, one of the teenagers was saying to another, "You're putting dirt into your mind!"

What is going into your mind? Chocolate or dirt? What is dirt for *your* mind?

PHILIPPIANS 4:8: SPIRITUAL VITAMINS

Just as our physical lives are sustained and protected by the vitamins we take in from our food, our spiritual lives are affected by what we take in from the world outside ourselves. Taking in that which the apostle Paul describes in Philippians 4:8—those things that are true and right and noble and pure, those things that cause us to act in ways that inspire others and call forth love—causes our spiritual selves to grow and flourish. We grow closer and closer to Jesus as we act more and more as he acted when he lived among us.

SPIRITUAL NUTRITION

Questions to help you choose your spiritual vitamins

What kind of books do you like to read?

What are you reading now (or have read in the last two months)?

What magazines do you subscribe to or read regularly?

What television shows do you watch regularly? (As my sister-in-law says, "What is your must-see TV?")

What DVDs or videos are you watching?

What music do you listen to (CDs, radio, MP3 player)?

What music is in your CD player (home and vehicles) right now? What music is on your MP3 player?

If you have a computer, go to the "history" tab on your internet server home page at home. List the websites you visited yesterday. (Do this survey on all the computers you own.)

PHILIPPIANS 4:8: SPIRITUAL VITAMINS

The day before yesterday.

Do any of the things you watch, listen to, or see bother you in any way? Do you ever think, "There is something wrong about doing this"? Be honest with yourself.

Ask the same question during your prayer time and listen for the answer.

> ### The Dollar Diet
>
> During a financial planning class, the teacher advised everyone to take the "dollar diet." She suggested that we write down everything we bought for a month no matter how small the cost. Then look at our list. Spending $50 a month on lattes? $200 a month on lunches?
>
> Try a spiritual "dollar diet." Write down everything you read, watch, or listen to, the Web sites you visit and the video games you play for a month. After a month take the list to your prayer time and look at it. Would you be proud to show the list to your pastor or to a Christian friend? Do you need to make some changes?

MISSING NUTRIENTS?

CHAPTER 10

> [They] brought bedding and bowls and articles of pottery. They also brought wheat and barley, flour and roasted grain, beans and lentils, honey and curds, sheep, and cheese from cows' milk for David and his people to eat. For they said, "The people have become hungry and tired and thirsty in the desert."
> —2 Samuel 17:28–9

> Do not forget to do good and to share with others, for with such sacrifices God is pleased.
> —Hebrews 13:16

The first time I shared the concept of spiritual nutrients, I asked everyone to write down what they thought were the five most important spiritual nutrients. After I had presented my list, several people were unhappy. "You left out _____." I replied, "No, I didn't."

Three practices that others have most often suggested should be spiritual nutrients are love, giving, and service. I have given much thought, prayer, and study to these three. I believe

SPIRITUAL NUTRITION

that if our spiritual lives are strong in the five core spiritual nutrients—prayer, Bible study, Christian fellowship, worship, and filling our minds with the good things listed in Philippians 4:8—we will love as Jesus loves. We will have the heart of Jesus, who came down from the Mount of Transfiguration to serve the people in the crowd who waited for him (Luke 9:37–42). We will give and serve from a heart that is grateful for all God has done for us.

Upon years of reflection and observation, this belief seems overly hopeful. There are people who eat well and carefully but who have little social life, do not exercise, or do not have much mental stimulation. Are these people "healthy"? In the same way, there are people who have all five core spiritual nutrients in their lives in at least some degree, but do not live the life that Jesus desires for those who follow him. They do not show the heart of Jesus in what they say and do.

Although love, giving, serving, and other fruits of a life filled with Jesus Christ should flow naturally out of a healthy spiritual life, sometimes they do not.

Different nutritional needs

Our bodies' needs

Individuals have different nutritional needs for their physical bodies. For example,

- Pregnant women need to ensure that they have enough folic acid in their diets (to protect against birth defects), extra protein, and may need additional vitamins and minerals.

MISSING NUTRIENTS?

- Nursing mothers need additional water, calories, minerals, and vitamins.[28]
- Some medications may cause less efficient processing of nutrients in the foods we eat. Some foods may cause the medications we take to be less effective.
- Those who are involved in strenuous sports need more water to replenish water lost in perspiration, more carbohydrates for energy, and more protein to build muscles (depending on their sport).

Our spirits' needs

Because of our personal situations we may need to focus on one of the five spiritual nutrients. Each of us may need a little less of one nutrient or more of one or more nutrients. We may need to focus on another nutrient for our spiritual health. Physical bodies are different. Spiritual hearts are different. We let God speak to our hearts about what we may need to add to the basic five spiritual nutrients.

Love, giving, and service

We will consider love, giving, and service as three additional nutrients that we may need to add to our spiritual diets. We can also think of these nutrients as exercise for our spirits.

Love

Several people over the years have insisted that the list of the five nutrients must include love. I believe that the love we have for one another flows from Jesus Christ living in us. Jesus' love will flow from his heart through us.

SPIRITUAL NUTRITION

Because love for others comes from the love of Jesus flowing through our hearts, we cannot love others if our heart is blocked or hardened. To unblock our hearts so that we can love others we must make sure that the core spiritual nutrients are present in our lives in adequate measure. When we practice good spiritual nutrition, we keep our eyes on Jesus and not on ourselves.

The book of 1 John gives us practical ways to know if the love of Jesus is flowing through our lives. In 1 John 4:21, we read, "Whoever loves God must also love his brother [or sister]."

Read 1 John 3:14–18. How does John say that we show love to one another?

1. If we hate another believer, we do not love (e.g., 1 John 2:9; 3:15). We are good at rationalizing this teaching: "I don't hate him. I just don't like him very much."
2. We are willing to lay down our lives for each other, just as Jesus laid down his life for us (v. 16). How do we "lay down our lives" for another short of throwing ourselves in front of a car that is about to hit someone else?
3. John says that if we have material possessions and another believer is in need of what we have, the love of Jesus in us compels us to help the other. We must have the desire, even the compulsion, to share what we have with others who are in need. The desire to give must result not only in wanting to give but also in giving (vv. 17–18).
4. We do not just say how much we love another but we do something about it. We love "with actions and in truth" (v. 18).

Dump trucks and deviled eggs

We all know believers who regularly attend worship, Bible studies, pray, and interact with other Christians but do not love.

Have you ever met another believer who used what I call "dump trucking"? Whenever I perceive that someone has done something wrong to me, I store my feelings in an imaginary dump truck. When the dump truck is full, perhaps years later, I just let it all dump out on the "offensive" person. In an angry outburst I ask, "Remember when you stepped on my foot in kindergarten? And then when you stole my homework in second grade? And when you went out with my boyfriend in seventh grade?" Of course you don't remember. You just know that all that stuff pouring on you hurts.[29]

If you have ever attended a small church, this story will be familiar to you. Betty always brings deviled eggs to church suppers. One night, Jane, who has just started attending the church, brings deviled eggs to a church supper. Betty says, "I'll never forgive her for bringing deviled eggs. *I* always bring the deviled eggs." Betty means it. This is a true story. Only the food has been changed to protect the innocent.

We show love for one another—or the lack of love—by our actions.

More than a feeling

Sometimes we just have to love each other, even when we don't feel like it. Some people are hard to love because they seem to repel any effort we make to reach out to them. When it's hard to love someone else, we must act toward that person as if we did love her or him.

One hears the advice that if a person does not feel love toward one's spouse, one should act as if the love were present. Do what one did when dating or first married. Bring or send

SPIRITUAL NUTRITION

flowers. Go out for a nice dinner. Speak kind words and do kind things for your spouse. Doing loving things may result in a return of the love that once was present between husband and wife. Sometimes actions can create feelings.

One day I was riding the city bus during the middle of the day. I looked around the bus at the other people. Some were well dressed for work, like me. Some wore dirty, rumpled clothes and smelled like they needed clean underwear. One, hunched over, in layers of mismatched clothes and a dirty stocking cap, muttered to herself. Some were elderly. Some were young. In the back of the bus, a teenager with green hair and an attitude roughhoused with his friends with attitudes. It hit me like a punch—Jesus loves every person on this bus as much as he loves me. How, then, can I judge that anyone is unworthy of my love?

In 1 John, John is telling us that how we love one another reflects how much we love God. To put it another way, we love God only as much as we love the person we love the least.

Giving

In this section we are looking at giving money to the local church in which we worship.

It may seem like the church is always asking for money. "The church" is the body of Christ in a particular place that is seeking to be the presence of Jesus in its place and time. To be the presence of Jesus, money is required for salaries, renting space, buying crayons, paper and furniture for children, licenses for music, and utilities.

The spirit of giving that God asks from us

Some people give to reward God—tossing a large bill in the offering plate—whenever they feel that God has been good to them. The fallacy of this way of giving is that God is always good to us. All that we have belongs to God and is a gift from God. Giving reminds us that it is not our efforts but God's goodness that has given us our houses, cars, food, sources of income, and bank accounts.

We give to please God, not because we are being forced to give, but cheerfully (2 Corinthians 9:7). God has made us rich "in every way" so that we can be generous. When we are generous God will receive thanksgiving (2 Corinthians 9:11). The world tells us that what we have is because of our efforts and we need to close our hand or someone will take what is ours. At the very least we want to get credit for our giving.

We must always be aware of the tension between God's free gifts and the world's words—"You earned it. It's yours." Giving reminds us of the incredible generosity of God to us, every moment of every day.

But I need all the money I can get

In the Old Testament, Moses calls the Israelites and us to the right use of our money. In the retelling of the story of the Israelites just before they crossed the Jordan into the Promised Land, Moses reminds the people that they must give to the poor. "If there is a poor man among your brothers in any of the towns of the land that the LORD your God is giving you, do not be hardhearted or tightfisted toward your poor brother. Rather be openhanded and freely lend him whatever he needs" (Deuteronomy 15:7–8).

Sometimes we must open our hands when our hearts tell us to keep our money in a tight fist. After all, economic times are tough. After all, we are nearing retirement. After all, we really need a new car. After all, I live on a "fixed income." Our hands close when our attitude is, after all, it's all about us.

God tells us to open our hands because our lives are all about God. A chapter subheading in the book, *Giving—The*

Sacred Art: Creating a Lifestyle of Generosity, is "Actions Lead to Feelings Lead to Transformation." Just as with love, when we give, God will grow in us the desire to give. The desire to give will transform our hearts. The author, Lauren Tyler Wright, points out that giving because God asks us to "is allowing God to shape us."[30]

Sometimes, we have to give, whether we want to or not, because we need the exercise. We can't wait until we feel cheerful about it. When we give to honor God, God will create a cheerful heart in us.

What is tithing?

Tithing is giving ten percent of our income to the local church in which we worship.

In church bulletins before the offering time we may see the phrase, "tithes and offerings." Offerings are gifts we give in addition to the ten percent we give to the church. First the tithes, then the offerings. Offerings can be given for church projects or to Christian organizations.

Some people believe that the tithe, giving one-tenth of one's income, was only for people who lived in the Old Testament days. In Leviticus 27:30, God told the people of Israel that a tithe of "everything from the land"—crops and animals—belongs to God. Tithes were given as the salary of the priests, who could not raise crops or animals because their job was to serve in the temple (Numbers 18:21).

However, Jesus never said, "About the tithe? You can forget it now that I'm here."

For me, the tithe is an important discipline.[31] My tithe is the first item of my budget. I consider a tenth of my monthly income God's money, not mine. For me to keep this ten percent would be to steal from God, an action I want to avoid. (In Malachi 3:6–10 God tells the people of Israel that when they did not bring the whole tithe they were robbing God.) Time and again, one hears stories of a family who stopped tithing when times got rough. After they stopped tithing times got rougher. When they began to tithe again their circumstances changed.

Tithing is not magic. Tithing affects the heart of the believer and reminds us that all that we have is God's gift to us.

If we have a grudging attitude toward giving, we need to take that attitude to God in prayer, study what the Bible says about giving, and ask other believers to hold us accountable. When we think on all that we have as a gift from God as we give our money during worship services God can grow in us the attitude toward money he desires us to have.

Service

Richard Foster describes service as a spiritual discipline in his book *Celebration of Discipline*. The service Foster describes is a heart attitude of serving others. Service as we will consider it here is actions we take outside the local church building to meet needs in our communities and in our world (with the heart attitude of serving).

Jesus describes service outside the community of believers in Matthew 25:35–36: "For I was hungry and you gave me something to eat, I was thirsty and you gave me something to drink, I was a stranger and you invited me in, I needed clothes and you clothed me, I was sick and you looked after me, I was in prison and you came to visit me." When we serve others outside our body of believers we serve Jesus, himself (Matthew 25:40).

When we give and serve, God will not give us awards or merit badges or medals. We serve because, through our prayer, Bible study, Christian fellowship, worship, and thinking on good things we have the heart and mind of Jesus who "did not come to be served but to serve" (Matthew 20:28).

We give out of hearts filled with the love of Jesus Christ, who gave his life so that we might live and, in turn, give our lives for the world. Spiritual director and author Brennan Manning, using the example of Mother Teresa, says that service "embodies the mind of Christ."[32]

Love, giving, and service are like exercise

When we would rather spit on another person or try to get even for a perceived slight, we need to grit our teeth and act in love. When we feel our hands clutching, we need to give. Sometimes we need to get out of our little lives and into the world and serve. Loving, giving, and serving exercise our spiritual hearts just as walking, biking, or working out exercise our physical hearts. Like exercise, which gives us sore muscles at first, the more we do the more we can do and want to do.

Being spiritual couch potatoes, even if we are reading the Bible while we lie on the couch, leads to a hardened heart and a closed hand toward others, which will eventually create a hardened heart toward God.

Questions to consider

How much did you give to charities last year?
To which organizations did you give? How did you choose them?

Do you have a giving plan?
>   For example, do you tithe?
>   Do you give a certain amount each month to charities or to the church?
>   Do you always give to the same charities?
>   How do you choose the charities you give to?
>   Do you give to your local church?
>   Do you give to Christian organizations?
>   What is your giving plan?

If you don't give, why not?

If you do give, why do you give?

What volunteer organizations do you belong to? What do they do and what do you do in them?

SPIRITUAL NUTRITION

Why do you choose to serve the way you do?

If you don't serve others in your community, why don't you?

> Choose an organization and investigate opportunities for service.

A BALANCED DIET

CHAPTER 11

[The believers] devoted themselves to the apostles' teaching and to the fellowship, to the breaking of bread and to prayer.
—Acts 2:42

Nutrients in food work together

Each nutrient depends on the presence of other nutrients to do its work.[33]

A concept that explores the interaction of foods is "food synergy." "Synergy" means that when two or more things interact, the whole is greater than any of the individual parts. Although how nutrients work together is a developing science, food scientists know that when certain foods are eaten together greater health benefits result than when the same foods are eaten separately or with other foods.[34]

Our bodies need all the vitamins, minerals, and other compounds found in foods. Foods like citrus fruits that have vitamin

SPIRITUAL NUTRITION

C may have a little iron and calcium but not as much as our bodies need. Eggs do not have any vitamin C. We need to eat a variety of foods every day because no one food has all the nutrients we need.

The nutrients in our food work together. We need all of the nutrients every day to enable our physical bodies to function optimally.

Spiritual nutrients work together

Just as the nutrients in our food work together, the spiritual nutrients work together.

Bible study and prayer

Bible study is most effective when combined with prayer. When we study a passage in the Bible, the best way to begin our study is to pray for the Holy Spirit to show us what we need to learn from the passage.

Psalm 119

In Psalm 119, we see the absolute necessity of combining prayer and Bible study. For example, in verses 145–46, the psalmist says, "I call with all my heart; answer me, O Lord, and I will obey your decrees. I call out to you; save me and I will keep your statutes." It is only through the study of God's Word that we know, in our heads, at least, what the decrees and statutes of God are. The gift of God, given to us through prayer (our "calls to God"), is that our head knowledge of God's laws becomes heart knowledge. We come to understand that the decrees of God are wise and are not given just to annoy us. Through prayer, we are given God's strength to do what God desires of us. "May my cry come before you, O Lord; give me understanding according to your word" (Psalm 119:169). We pray for understanding of the Word that we study.

Daniel 9

In Daniel 9, Daniel prays for the Israelites in exile in Babylon. Daniel's prayer was made in response to Scripture: "I, Daniel, understood from the Scriptures, according to the word of the Lord given to Jeremiah the prophet, that the desolation of Jerusalem would last seventy years" (Daniel 9:2). Prayer and God's Word are intertwined.

Christian fellowship

We experience Christian fellowship when we pray for each other, study the Bible together, worship together, encourage each other, and hold each other accountable for thinking on good things.

Studying the Bible together helps us stay on the right track in our interpretation and application of God's Word. Morning Bible study with others starts our day grounded in Jesus Christ.

Group Bible study can easily be combined with praying together.

AN IDEA FOR YOUR BIBLE STUDY GROUP

In one weekly Bible study group, the group ends with each person taking a note card. Each person writes his or her name, a praise, and a prayer request on the card. The cards are randomly passed out to the group members and read by the one who has the card. Each person has someone praying for him or her for the whole week.

SPIRITUAL NUTRITION

Corporate worship

The Bible is important in worship—the reading of God's Word, preaching from Scripture, and singing hymns and praise songs based on Scripture.

Even if your church prints the Bible passages for the day in the bulletin or on a screen, it helps to bring your own Bible to look up the passages. You will become more familiar with your Bible and you can mark the passages for later reading and study.

Prayer is an important part of corporate worship. Many parts of a worship service involve prayer—invoking God's presence at the beginning of the service, prayers of intercession and praise, and the prayer of sending out (the benediction).

During worship, our minds can focus on the good things of God (although our minds can go astray, as well, just as they do at other times).

Thinking on good things

Focusing on what is good, true, and uplifting helps us to gain the most from corporate worship, prayer, Bible study, and Christian fellowship.

Prayer is an important element in Paul's admonition to think on things that are good and true. The instructions for thinking on good things in Philippians 4:8 follow an instruction on prayer: "In everything, by prayer and petition, with thanksgiving, present your requests to God" (Philippians 4:6). Prayer gives us God's peace (Philippians 4:7). Through prayer, God shows us what is right or wrong for us to do. The world calls it "conscience." Christians call such leading the voice of the Holy Spirit.

We have seen that prayer is as important to our spiritual health as water is to our physical health. Prayer is especially important to the spiritual health of our minds. The water we drink helps remove the waste created by our bodily functioning. The living water of prayer helps us to flush out toxic thoughts that want to stay in and poison our minds.

As we noted in chapter nine, "Spiritual Vitamins," Bible study—feeding on God's Word—helps us recognize what is healthful and what is harmful to put into our minds.

Christians need all the spiritual nutrients to be spiritually healthy. Although I have separated each of the five essential (core) nutrients, such a separation is only for the purposes of discussion. Prayer, Bible study, worship, Christian fellowship, and what we put into our minds are all bound together as we are bound together with other believers and with Jesus Christ. Good spiritual nutrition requires that we take in each spiritual nutrient every day of our lives.

SPIRITUAL NUTRITION

How balanced is your diet?

Do you know how many calories you should eat each day?
Go to *mypyramid.gov*, click "MyPyramid Plan" on the left and see.

Look at the Spiritual Nutrition Pyramid. Draw the pyramid as it represents your own spiritual life now. (Too much Christian fellowship? Not much Bible study?)

Where do you need to improve?

Look up Acts 2:42–47.
Which spiritual nutrients did the disciples have in their lives?

Which of the spiritual nutrients in their lives are present in your life?

Which spiritual nutrients would you like to have more of?

What could you do today to start including these nutrients in your life?

MORE NUTRIENTS WITH LESS EFFORT

CHAPTER 12

Work smarter not harder.

Food

When we combine foods from different food groups (what MyPyramid calls "mixed dishes") we get more nutrients with less effort. Celery sticks or apple slices with peanut butter give us carbohydrates, fiber, vitamins, protein, and healthy fats. A sandwich can include bread, meat, cheese, and vegetables for a nearly all-inclusive nutritional package.

Warning

When eating mixed dishes, we must be careful about unhealthy fat and sugars and the amount of healthy fats that we may be eating. For example, pizza has many different nutrients in the crust, tomato sauce, vegetables, meats, and cheeses. But the pizza can be loaded with high-fat meats, such as pepperoni and sausage, and lots of whole milk cheese. A more healthy choice—make the

SPIRITUAL NUTRITION

pizza at home, use a thin crust and put on lots of vegetables and a minimal amount of low-fat mozzarella cheese.

We can make a sandwich with white bread, lots of regular mayonnaise, butter, high-fat processed meats, and cheese made from whole milk. A healthier mix of nutrients would be a sandwich with whole wheat bread, low-fat mayonnaise, mustard, lots of vegetables, and a small amount of low-fat meat and low-fat or non-fat cheese.

Spiritual food

Corporate worship

We can take in more nutrients with less effort by attending a worship service. There we will receive all of the nutrients: prayer, Bible reading and the fruits of Bible study from the sermon, Christian fellowship, thinking on good things, and giving.

Bible study

Attending a Bible study with other Christians also provides many spiritual nutrients: we pray for our study and can have a time to pray for each other; we study the Bible before we meet; we have a chance to share our ideas about the passage we are studying; we experience Christian fellowship; and we think on good things. Some groups will also do service projects together in the community or give to provide food, shelter, or clothing to those in need.

Warning

Worship services. When we attend worship services, a main motivation can be to see our friends rather than to worship.

MORE NUTRIENTS WITH LESS EFFORT

Have you ever been to a church worship service for the first time and had someone (maybe even the pastor) lean over you to talk to a friend, ignoring you as if you were not sitting there? Sometimes when I go to a new church I feel like going outside to see if there is a "Members Only" sign and the greeter (who didn't speak to me, either) was just too polite to tell me I couldn't come in. One of my dreams is to be a part of a church where people come to worship expecting to see new people they can welcome. When I attend a worship service, I look for and introduce myself to people who are new to the church. I don't wait for the pastor to tell me to greet someone.

Sometimes people say, "I'm no good at meeting people. That's a job for the greeters." Anyone can look someone in the eye and smile. Smiling shows that we see the other person instead of looking through her to find someone we know. It is also easy to say, "Have we met?" Be careful if you have trouble with names. In one church someone told me, "After the greeter asked me for the twelfth time, 'Have we met?' I decided to go somewhere else." If you aren't good at remembering faces, stick to the smile.

It is helpful for us to pray on the night before the worship service for God to open our eyes to those we need to meet and to make our worship experience a gift to God instead of simply an opportunity for visiting with our friends.

Study groups. We know that the temptation when we gather with others is to tell stories on other people—that is, to gossip. Although we seem to enjoy sharing the faults in others, thinking on the faults of others is not thinking on good things. We need to monitor our own hearts, minds, and mouths as well as holding each other accountable for what comes out of our mouths. A simple rule (simple to say, not to do) is if what we want to say might be gossip—don't say it.

SPIRITUAL NUTRITION

Questions for reflection

Look at the next sandwich you make. How could you make the sandwich healthier?

Attend a worship service in a church where you don't know anyone.
    Did you see anyone in the parking lot? Did they greet you?

Who greeted you inside the church building? Was there a greeter? Was he or she friendly or did you feel like they were just doing their job?

How did you feel about your experience?

What did you learn that you could do to make your church more welcoming? What will you do at this week's worship service?

Anticipate that you will see someone you don't know. Look for that person or that family. Smile. Invite them to your fellowship time after worship.

Talk about gossip in your Bible study, ministry, or fellowship group. How does your group define gossip? How are you going to hold each other accountable for not gossiping when the group is together?

I'M READY TO MAKE SOME CHANGES— NOW WHAT DO I DO?

CHAPTER 13

> No matter how small the step in the right direction, gradual improvement to one's health can be made.
> —MyPyramid Peer to Peer.ppt

> Commit to the Lord whatever you do, and your plans will succeed.
> —Proverbs 16:3

What do you do if you know you need better spiritual nutrition? How can you change habits that are so familiar?

Prayer

The best first step is to pray, asking God for courage, understanding, wisdom, and strength to change a spiritual bad habit.

One day long ago when I was a camper at a high school summer church camp, I asked the leaders of a group what I should do about an unpleasant girl who had decided to be my shadow in school. I said, "And don't just tell me to pray about it." What I meant was that I did not want an easy answer with no practical help. As I recall, the leaders looked at each other with blank stares. They had no answer other than "pray about it" so they stood there, silent. Being a young believer, I did not understand that prayer was the way to begin to change my own heart about the person involved and to see her with the eyes of Jesus. All I knew then was that I had heard too much dismissal from adults in "just pray about it."

Prayer is the first step to a changed heart and a changed life. Pray first and ask others to pray with and for you. Consider the practical advice below.

Attitude

Changing unhealthy spiritual habits is no different from changing unhealthy physical habits such as smoking or eating too much sugar. We have to want to change.

The book, *Healthy Weight for EveryBody* published by the Mayo Clinic, stresses the importance of attitude in developing healthy eating habits. If we are going to change bad habits to healthy habits, we must understand the challenges we face and that change is going to take time, patience, and a plan.[35] In the same way, changing our spiritual habits requires carefully considering obstacles to change and a plan to keep those obstacles from preventing us from reaching our goal of becoming spiritually healthy.

Take small steps

It is important to work toward an overall goal for better physical or spiritual health. We will have a better chance of reaching our long-term goal when we identify, write down, and share our goal and move toward the goal with short-term goals we know we can reach. Small successes are the path to great rewards.

I'M READY TO MAKE SOME CHANGES—NOW WHAT DO I DO?

Putting change into practice

As an example, here is a series of steps to take to make more time for prayer.

- **Begin to change by praying.** Praise and thank God. Tell God that you want to set aside more time for prayer but that you can't possibly find one more minute in your day. Ask for God's guidance.
- **Listen for God's answer** in the voice of the Holy Spirit. Think about what times you have free in your day or can make free for prayer. Talk with your family about your desire to pray more often. Talk with them about how they can help you have some time to pray when and where you won't be disturbed.
- **Set goals.** Don't decide to pray every day, at first. Write down a specific overall goal. Start your journey toward your overall goal with small goals, such as praying at a regular time once a week, maybe on Saturday evening. If your prayer time is on Saturday evening and your worship service is the next day, you can pray for your pastor and worship leaders and everyone that God will lead to the service. You can pray for those who will come who have never been in church before. (If your worship service is on a Saturday, begin praying on Friday evenings.) Set an amount of time to pray, even five or ten minutes at first. Use a timer so that if you run out of words, you will at least sit quietly without wondering how much more time you have to sit there.
- **Pick a quiet place** to pray—not in front of the TV or computer! Some people have a "prayer chair" where they sit to pray. I have made a little area in the corner of our guest bedroom with a small stool, a candle, some pictures, and a few special objects.

SPIRITUAL NUTRITION

- As suggested above, **begin** praying once a week for five to ten minutes.
- **Use a notebook or journal** to record your goals and your progress. Note the days you prayed. Did the amount of time seem long enough? Too long? Were you interrupted or distracted? Write down anything that seems important to reaching your goal.
- After several weeks, **review your progress.** Change the place or time if the original place or time isn't working out. Add minutes or days to your prayer time. Review your journal. Are you closer to your overall goal? Share your goals and progress with a Christian friend who will encourage you.
- **Oops!** If you go out one Saturday night and forget to have your prayer time, don't beat yourself up for it. Note your "oops" in your journal. Either pray another time that week or make sure you are intentional about your next prayer time. (Like the label on prescription medication bottles says, if you forget to take a pill, take it when you remember it or just skip that missed day!) Maybe the time doesn't work or the place isn't conducive to prayer. If the desire of your heart is to grow closer to God through prayer, God will help you find times and a place to set aside for prayer.
- **Let others help you.** Put your Christian fellowship into action. Talk with your Christian friends about how you are trying to improve your spiritual health. Ask a friend to pray with you and for you. Ask a friend to have Bible study with you. Just like exercising with someone else helps us keep our commitment to exercise, praying or studying the Bible with someone else will help us pray and study. You might be surprised how eager your friends will be to work on their own spiritual health.

I'M READY TO MAKE SOME CHANGES—NOW WHAT DO I DO?

The more we develop new habits, the more we want to do. When we open our hearts to God in willingness to grow in faith and love, God will take advantage of our willingness and open our hearts even more. All it takes is turning to God with a heart desire to change.

We may go too far in trying to establish a new spiritual habit. When we diet, we may lose too much weight and develop physical problems or the diet we choose may be unhealthy. In the same way, we can overdo spiritually. We can try to do too much too fast and end up burned out. Two keys to developing healthy spiritual habits are patience and prayer.

To create lasting change and lasting growth, we listen to God. We listen to our Christian friends. It takes time to develop the habits that lead to good spiritual health. **You can do it** with the power and strength God provides through the Holy Spirit and the encouragement of other Christians.

Questions to help you put your desire to be spiritually healthy into practice

As you consider the list of spiritual nutrients, is there one or more that you need more of in your spiritual diet?

Choose one _____
What are you doing now on this element?

What would you like to do?

SPIRITUAL NUTRITION

What steps can you take in the next week to begin to work on your goal?

Write your goal and the steps you are going to take in the next week in a notebook.

On a calendar, make an appointment with yourself in one week to look at the steps you were going to take.

Did you take the steps you wrote down? If not, why not?

Do you need to modify your plan?

If you took the steps you wanted to take what happened?

What is your next step? (It may be to keep doing step one.)

Make the same appointment with yourself every week. Write the answers in your notebook every week.

Thank God in prayer for helping you set a goal and for the strength to keep working toward better spiritual health.

> May the God of peace . . . equip you with everything good for doing his will, and may he work in us what is pleasing to him, through Jesus Christ.
> —Hebrews 13:20–21

HOW TO MAKE IT HAPPEN

Ten Ways to Improve Your Spiritual Nutrition

1. Praise God every day (because God is great, for your job, your family, a beautiful sunset). Look for ways to praise God all day for the things in your day.
2. Give thanks to God before you begin to eat each meal.
3. Purchase a Bible that is written in a way that you can understand and helps you understand the Scriptures you read.
4. Read in your Bible every day. Write down your times for Bible study as appointments on your calendar and keep the appointments.
5. Watch movies or television shows that make you laugh, teach you, help you understand the world, and promote compassion for others.
6. Create (and use) a playlist of Christian songs for your MP3 player.
   In addition to a "Christian songs" playlist, I have an "Encouragement" playlist of Christian songs that help me to keep putting one foot in front of the other.

SPIRITUAL NUTRITION

7. Regularly encourage your Christian friends and relatives with e-mails, text messages, cards, or calls.
8. Choose a local non-profit group. Call or e-mail the group's office and get involved, with time and/or monetary support.
9. Give to the church you attend regularly.
10. Visit other churches when you travel. Attend a worship service, a prayer group, or a Bible study.

[In one church, we brought bulletins from the churches we attended on our summer vacations and put them on the bulletin board. We make a map of all the places people had worshipped that summer.]

Meeting Our Minimum Spiritual Nutrition Needs

- Pray every day.
  Include ten minutes of uninterrupted prayer at least three times a week.
  Pray with other Christians at least twice a week.
- Read from the Bible every day.
  Study more in-depth (including looking up maps or words) three times a week.
  Study with others at least twice a month.
- Connect with other Christians at least once a day.
- Have an attitude of worship every day.
  Worship with others at least twice a month.
- Think on good things every day.
- Look for and practice ways to serve people in need.

HOW TO MAKE IT HAPPEN

My Personal Spiritual Meal Plan

Morning

- Before I get out of bed, I ask Jesus to help me be the person he wants me to be today. If I have any difficult tasks, I ask Jesus to be with me during them. I focus on the love of Jesus flowing through me. Then I get up.
- I read a portion of the NIV version of *The One Year Bible*, either the Old Testament verse and psalm or the New Testament verse. If I am drawn to a particular part of what I read, I focus on it.
- If I am working at home, I sit quietly in God's presence before I begin work. I listen to a Christian podcast devotional or song before I begin work.

Evening

- We give thanks for our evening meal.
- I am careful about what I watch on evening television, especially just before bed. I read in a spiritual book just prior to going to sleep.
- I try to have a prayer time between 9:00 and 9:30 P.M.

Preparation for worship

- On Saturday evenings, I spend the evening quietly if I can, reading in a spiritual book and listening to Christian music. As we prepare breakfast on Sunday morning, we put on a Christian CD as background music. We turn to a Christian radio station as we drive to the worship service.

SPIRITUAL NUTRITION

A Week of Menu Ideas to Implement your Spiritual Nutrition Needs

The Importance of a Good Breakfast

A healthy breakfast, such as a bowl of cereal with low-fat milk and fruit or a poached egg, whole wheat toast, and fruit, gives us the stamina and energy for our morning's activities. We will also eat less (the doughnuts our thoughtful co-workers bring, candy bars, high-fat lunches) during the day if we start the day with breakfast.

In the same way, when we start the day with spiritual food, we have the stamina and energy to live for Jesus throughout the day. Our minds will begin the day centered on Jesus and be less prone to being influenced by unhealthy thoughts.

Sing a praise song in the shower, tape a Bible verse to your mirror to ponder as you shave or put on make-up, put a Bible verse in your backpack or briefcase where you will see it, say a prayer with someone in your family before you go off to work or school, look at a devotional for the day while you eat your cereal, go to a Bible study group before work, or try one of the menu ideas below.

Be creative!

HOW TO MAKE IT HAPPEN

Day One

Morning

- Start the day with praise and thanksgiving for a new day. Ask for courage and the understanding of what God would have you do today. You can do this before you get out of bed.

Afternoon

- If you go out for lunch, sing a praise song or hymn to yourself as you walk. If you make lunch at home, sing while you prepare the meal.
- Give thanks for your meal and for those who share it with you.

Evening

- End the day with a prayer of thanks for the day.
- Read a brief Bible passage in bed before you turn off the light.

Tips for day one

Praise songs

Don't know any praise songs? Any song is a good one to start with, including "Jesus Loves Me." If you have children or special children in your life who attend a church group (such as Awana, Sunday school, vacation Bible school, or a midweek church program), they can teach you some of the songs they know. The staff at a Christian bookstore can help you choose a CD of easy praise songs that can help you learn some songs that speak to your heart.

SPIRITUAL NUTRITION

Or you can sing any chorus of a hymn that you know. Looking through a hymn book or listening to hymns might help jog your memory.

Suggested Bible passages for bedtime reading

John 14:27
Psalm 23
Philippians 4:8–9
Psalm 4:8
Romans 5:1–2

Psalm 62:1–2
1 John 3:1–3
Romans 15:13
Psalm 131
Isaiah 26:3–4

Day Two

Morning

- Give thanks for your meal and for those who share it with you. Do this even though you just "eat and run."

Afternoon

- Say an encouraging word to a Christian co-worker. Call, write, text, or e-mail a Christian friend (or your pastor) with a word of encouragement.
- If you are home, watch a Christian television program instead of one of your regular programs. (Just for today!)

Evening

- Load your MP3 player with Christian music to listen to tomorrow or set out Christian tapes or CDs to listen to tomorrow.

Tips for day two

Encouragement

As we saw in the chapter on Christian fellowship, believers can encourage one another to stand fast when things are tough. Think of those you know who are being treated for cancer or other illnesses, who are depressed, or who are facing difficult decisions. Encourage them with a card, e-mail, or phone call.

Tell someone you are thinking about her and praying for her. Tell someone how special he is in your life or how he has helped you.

Day Three

Morning

- Listen to Christian music on your commute or as you work at home.

Afternoon

- Go outside or, if it's too cold, look outside at a mountain, river, flower, tree, or any natural object. Give thanks to God for creating it and for giving you the opportunity to see it and care for it.

Evening

- Give thanks for your meal and for those who share it with you.
- Find a Bible verse that encourages you. Write or type it and put it up on your bathroom mirror.
- Listen to Christian music before you go to bed or in your car as you travel to and from activities.

SPIRITUAL NUTRITION

- Let your last words of the evening be: "Thank you, Lord, for this day."

Tips for day three

Suggestions for encouraging Bible verses.

Think about how you need to be encouraged. Are you dealing with illness, money issues, toddlers or teenagers, work problems, or a church fight? Do you need a little push to implement a plan for better spiritual nutrition in your life? Use your concordance to look up verses that include the word "health," "children," "work," "money," "prayer," or any area in which you need encouragement. Share ideas with Christian friends.

Here are some verses you might use for encouragement:

1 Peter 1:6–9	Isaiah 12:2
Romans 15:13	Jeremiah 29:11–14
Psalm 37:1–7	Revelation 21:1–5
John 21:1–14	2 Chronicles 32:7–8
Deuteronomy 31:6–8	Psalm 34
Isaiah 40:25–31	Psalm 138:1–3
Psalm 27	

Day Four

Morning

- Read the verse you put on your mirror last night. Keep the verse on the mirror for the rest of the week (or longer) and read it as you get ready for work or ready for your day. Try to memorize it.

Afternoon

- If you work in a downtown area, buy someone who asks you for money a cup of coffee or a sandwich.
- If you are home select an item of food from your pantry or cupboard and set it aside for your local food bank.

Evening

- Give thanks for your meal and for those who share it with you.
- Listen to Christian music before you go to bed or in your car as you travel to and from activities.

Days Five and Six

Use ideas that worked for you in the past three days or ideas you have to pray, praise, encourage, support, read and study the Bible, worship, put good things into your mind, and share with others.

Think about which days and which times of day you could spend in ten minutes of prayer or Bible reading. Then, do it!

Tips for days five and six

How do I find ten minutes of time for myself?

Remember my friend who was so excited about doing Bible study that she announced she was going to start getting up at 5:00 A.M. and study? She worked full-time and had a husband and two energetic, school-aged boys. I cautioned her that maybe she was being a little unrealistic. She did want to keep up Bible study, didn't she?

SPIRITUAL NUTRITION

Do you think best in the morning or evening? Could you carve out some time at lunch, maybe even asking a co-worker or neighbor to study the Bible or pray with you during the day? Talk with your spouse and children about what would be a good time for you to set aside for study or prayer. If you are able to use a room at home for study or prayer, make a sign to hang on the door that says "Quiet! Prayer Zone" or "Dad's Praying" just to remind everyone that you are praying.

Day Seven (can be Saturday or Sunday)

- Attend a worship service. Listen to quiet music before the service and while you drive to the service.
- Spend the rest of the day enjoying your family or friends.
- Find a ten-minute block of time and a quiet place and sit quietly in God's presence. Listen and then share any needs that are on your heart.
- Refrain from watching violent movies or television shows or playing violent video games on this day.

HOW TO MAKE IT HAPPEN

Spiritual Nutrition for Special Situations

At Work

- If you have your own desk, keep a small Bible in a desk drawer.
  At one job, I had a small New Testament/Psalms in my top desk drawer. I would start the day and the afternoon by reading a psalm and praying.
- Know your employer's rules about wearing religious jewelry and playing religious radio programs. Respect these rules.
- If you are allowed to listen to your computer, MP3 player, or CD player with headphones, listen to Christian music or podcasts.
- Keep your ears open to identify other Christians in your workplace. (Often they will make a comment about "their church.") Make contact with them and ask for prayer when you need it.
- Pray for your boss and co-workers. Pray especially for any people that make your workplace difficult.
- If management permits it, start a Bible study or Christian book study group during your lunch hour. If it is not permitted, start one off the business premises.

Busy/Stressful Days

- Start your day centered in God. Take a few moments to breathe quietly. Thank God for being with you and for all the blessings you have.
- Play a Christian radio station or CDs in the car as you travel or at home.
- Take a moment to pray for your food before your meals.

SPIRITUAL NUTRITION

- End your day centered. Take a moment (perhaps before you brush your teeth) for a quiet prayer of thanks that you made it to the end of the day and for a restful night.

When You Are Sick

- *If you are home*
  - Play Christian music. Watch inspiring DVDs.
  - If you feel comfortable doing so, let someone know who can pray for you and ask others to pray.
- *If you are in the hospital*
  - Pack your Bible. Even if you can't read it, ask a visitor to read to you.
  You can also pack an easy-to-read Christian magazine or novel.
  - Listen to the playlists of Christian songs on your MP3 player.
  - Listen to Christian music CDs on a portable CD player.
  - Ask for a visit from the chaplain.
  - Call your pastor or ask the chaplain or a friend to call your pastor. Your pastor will want to pray for you and, hopefully, visit.

HOW TO MAKE IT HAPPEN

WHAT ARE YOUR SPIRITUAL COMFORT FOODS?

What is your favorite comfort food, food that just makes you feel good when you eat it? We turn to comfort food when we are stressed. Maybe your comfort food is macaroni and cheese, warm chocolate chip cookies, or hot chocolate with whipped cream.

List your favorite comfort foods.

_____
_____
_____

Think about your spiritual comfort food. What do think about when you are scared or under stress? Maybe you play or sing a special hymn or song or think of a special Bible passage, such as Psalm 23.

What are your spiritual "comfort foods"?

_____
_____
_____

When you feel stressed, go for your spiritual comfort food!

SPIRITUAL NUTRITION

When Traveling

- Before you leave, pray for yourself—for a good trip and safe travels. Ask God to keep you safe in your mind and heart while you are gone.
- If you do not want to pack your Bible, choose one or two passages and write them down. Put the verses in your suitcase and one in your purse or carry-on.
- If you are an early riser, begin the day by reading the passages you have copied. Pray for the day. Pray for your friends and family at home.
- End the day by reading the passage you have copied. Before you begin, ask God to teach you through the passage. You can write any insights on the paper on which the passage is printed.

   Give thanks for the day and for any specific events or people you met who are on your mind. Pray for your friends and family at home.
- If there are special prayer needs, such as a friend or relative who is having a medical test, surgery, or other important event while you will be gone, write down the name and what you want to pray for before you leave. Tape the prayer reminder in a prominent place in your hotel room so that you will remember to pray.
- Attend a worship service.
- Find a Christian station on your hotel television and have it on while you get ready to go out for the day.
- Prepare a Christian playlist for your MP3 player. Choose the Christian music that encourages you the most. Keep your MP3 player with your purse, briefcase, or bag and listen to your Christian playlist while you are in the airport, on the plane, bus, or train, during times when you have a break from meetings, and to help you relax before you go to bed.

HOW TO MAKE IT HAPPEN

- Download audio or video podcasts of your favorite preachers or Christian speakers. I like to watch a Joyce Meyer podcast on every leg of a plane trip. Propping my iPod on the lid of my glasses case gives me a movie-like view. On a recent trip as I was watching the podcast my seatmate pointed to her iPod. She was listening to a Joyce Meyer podcast, too!

Challenge

My vision for this book is that it will be a virus. A good virus, like the virus that is being tested to try to create new DNA in the body that will reverse the effects of Alzheimer's disease. My dream is that the virus that is this book will be used by the Holy Spirit to transform the church.

Do you believe that one person make a difference? Do you ever take a batch of cookies to share at work or a meeting? Make a difference by sharing this book. Take it to your pastor. Share it with your Christian friends, especially new believers. Take it to your Bible study or small group. Talk about it. Live it together.

In 2 Corinthians 3:18, the apostle Paul says that we are to be transformed into the likeness of Jesus. As the Holy Spirit begins to transform us, he will use us to transform the church. As our churches are transformed to live and act as the body of Christ, we will change the world.

I would love to know how you are doing and hear any ideas that have worked in your life to improve your spiritual nutrition. How has your Bible study or ministry group used the book? I am also planning a follow-up book that will explore more advanced spiritual practices such as fasting, centering prayer, and experiencing God in nature. What would you like to see in the book? Let me know at *christineprescott@rocketmail.com*.

RESOURCES

Nutrition

- *Nutrition for Dummies* by Carol Ann Rinzler, 4th ed. (2006)

    Easy to understand information about nutrition and food.

- *The Mayo Clinic Plan: 10 Essential Steps to a Better Body & Healthier Life*

    Includes all aspects of health, fitness, weight loss, and mental health, in addition to food and nutrition. It has lots of photographs and illustrations.

- *Eat, Drink, and Be Healthy: The Harvard Medical School Guide to Healthy Eating* by Walter Willett

Mary Jeanne recommends:

- *Tufts University Health & Nutrition Letter*

    Read more about this newsletter at *www.tuftshealthletter.com*.

SPIRITUAL NUTRITION

- *University of California, Berkeley, Wellness Letter*
    See *www.wellnessletter.com* for health information and information about the newsletter.
- *Nancy Clark's Sports Nutrition Guidebook* by Nancy Clark, MS, RD, 4th ed. (2008)
- *American Dietetic Association Complete Food and Nutrition Guide,* by Roberta Larson Duyff, 3rd ed. (2006).

Good Internet sources (not in order of importance) for finding up-to-date and accurate information on nutrition are:

- *www.mypyramid.gov*
    Audio and video podcasts about nutrition are available on the homepage of the website.
- MedlinePlus: *http://www.nlm.nih.gov/medlineplus/foodandnutrition.html*
- *www.mayoclinic.com* Includes a nutrition blog.
- The USDA Food and Nutritional Information Center, *http://nal.usda.gov/*
    The whole site is interesting. Click "Food and Nutrition" on the left side. Lots of links and lots of information.
- The American Dietetic Association: *www.eatright.org*
    Click the "Food and Nutrition Information" tab.
- The American Heart Association: *www.americanheart.org*
    Choose "Diet & Nutrition" from the "Healthy Lifestyle" tab. "Face the Fats" will help you learn more about healthy fats and get personalized recommendations.

RESOURCES

Prayer

Many books have been written about prayer. The books that have helped me are:

- *Prayer* by Richard Foster

    Describes fifteen different types of prayer. This is the best book on prayer that I have ever read.

- *About Quiet Prayer*

    A two-page booklet published by the Cathedral Center for Prayer and Pilgrimage of the Washington National Cathedral, Washington, D.C.

- *Prayer: Conversing With God* by Rosalind Rinker

    This was the first book I read about prayer. It helped me to understand that prayer was something I needed to do and could do.

- *Prayer* by Philip Yancey

    An exploration of prayer. Comprehensive resources list.

- *Living Peace* by John Dear

    In the first section of this book, Dear, a Jesuit priest, talks about the importance of time spent in solitude, silence, and listening to God.

- *Beginning to Pray* by Anthony Bloom

    Written by an Orthodox priest, this book is also excellent for those who are more experienced in prayer.

- *Too Busy Not to Pray* by Bill Hybels

    An easy-to-understand explanation of many aspects of prayer.

SPIRITUAL NUTRITION

Two books for those more confident in prayer:

- *Contemplative Prayer* by Thomas Merton
- *Centering Prayer* by M. Basil Pennington
    Pennington, who taught centering prayer, gives practical advice for praying the "Jesus Prayer."

Prayer collections

- *The Oxford Book of Prayer*
- *Laughter, Silence & Shouting: An Anthology of Women's Prayers* by Kathy Keay
- *Prayers from the Heart* by Richard Foster

Bible study

- *The Joy of Discovery in Bible Study* by Oletta Wald
    Either the first edition or the revised edition gives practical ideas for studying Bible passages and how to apply them to one's own life.
- *How to Read the Bible for All It's Worth* by Gordon Fee and Douglas Stuart
    This book by a New Testament scholar is now in its third edition. This book will help you understand the different types of Bible literature, the original meaning of Bible verses, and their application to your life today.
- *How to Read Your Bible* by David and Renée Sanford
    This book is especially designed to help a person read through the Bible from Genesis 1:1 to Revelation 22:21 (not even skipping Leviticus!). The book includes questions a person may have about the Bible, how to

RESOURCES

understand different types of Scriptures, and how to apply Scripture to one's life.

- *Using the Bible in Groups* by Roberta Hestenes

    Gives ideas for starting and leading a small group Bible study.

- *Meditating on the Word* by Dietrich Bonhoeffer

    Selections from Bonhoeffer's writing and thought that help us learn to read the Bible as a way "to meet Christ in his Word." Includes "A Meditation on Psalm 119."

- *Choosing a Bible* by Donald Kraus

    This book is for those who are interested in a more in-depth look at the various translations and versions of the Bible. The author compares the different Bibles available to chef's knives—each one is most useful for its intended purpose.

Christian fellowship

- *Life Together* by Dietrich Bonhoeffer

    From his personal experience living in a Christian community, Bonhoeffer discusses what it means for Christians to be in fellowship together.

- *Community and Growth* by Jean Vanier

    Vanier's reflection on Christian community from his experiences in the l'Arche community.

- *The Hilarity of Community* by Marva Dawn

    A study of Romans 12 that asks the question, "What would it be like if the Christian church were truly a community that thoroughly enjoyed being itself?"

SPIRITUAL NUTRITION

- *Connecting* by Larry Crabb

    How can believers provide encouragement to one another? While I think that many of Crabb's ideas are idealistic, this book encouraged me to believe in the power of Christians to help one another heal.

Worship

- Robert Webber wrote several books on worship including *Worship Is a Verb*. Any of Webber's books will be a good resource to learn more about any aspect of worship.

Love, Giving, and Service

- *Love As a Way of Life: Seven Keys to Transforming Every Aspect of Your Life* by Gary Chapman

    Practical ways to practice the habit of giving love. This book is also a great primer on thinking on good things. Chapman encourages us to think about how we can show love to others as we live our lives in the world and at home.

- *Giving—The Sacred Art: Creating a Lifestyle of Generosity* by Lauren Tyler Wright

    Includes a large section of resources and further reading on the subject of giving.

- Richard J. Foster and Kathryn A. Yanni discuss service as a spiritual discipline in *Celebration of Discipline and Celebrating the Disciplines: A Journal Workbook to Accompany Celebration of Discipline.*

RESOURCES

General Resources

- *Discipleship Journal's 101 Best Small-Group Ideas* compiled by Deena Davis

    Written for small groups, this book gives lots of ideas for starting and nourishing a small group and for prayer, Bible study, fellowship, service, and encouraging one another.

- *100 Ways to Simplify Your Life* by Joyce Meyer

    Short chapters with easy to implement ideas for making our lives spiritually healthy.

ENDNOTES

[1] All Bible quotations are from the NIV translation unless otherwise noted.

[2] "USDA's Food Guides: Background and Development" (Misc. Pub. #1514, USDA Human Nutrition Information Service, 1993), 3.

[3] Ibid., 33.

[4] See *www.mayoclinic.com/health/healthy-diet/NU00190* for a discussion of food pyramids.

[5] The nutrition information in the following chapters is based on information from *mypyramid.org* unless otherwise noted.

[6] Andrew Murray, *WITH CHRIST In the School of Prayer: Thoughts on Our Training for the Ministry of Intercession* (New York, NY: Fleming H. Revell Co., n.d.) 3.

[7] William McGee, "Protein in Diet," *www.nlm.nih.gov/medlineplus/ency/article/ 002467.htm*, 2007.

[8] Carol Ann Rinzler, *Nutrition for Dummies*, 4th ed. For Dummies series (Indianapolis, IN: Wiley Publishing, 2006), 70.

[9] Dietrich Bonhoeffer, *Meditating on the Word*, ed. and trans. David McI. Gracie (New York: Ballantine Books, 1986), 44–5. Epigraph at the beginning of the chapter, p. 111.

[10] While I was serving as a prison chaplain, I brought a young man a Bible as he had requested. He looked at it and said, "No. I want the original." Since the "originals" were written in Hebrew, Aramaic, and Greek, I asked (knowing the answer), "Oh. Do you read Hebrew and Greek?" He sheepishly said, "Well, no, not that original." He wanted a King James version that said, "The Authorized Version" on the title page. The "authorized" version was authorized by King James and is a translation of the originals, as they were known at that time.

[11] *Nutrition for Dummies*, 78.

[12] Dietrich Bonhoeffer says that those separated from the community of believers understand that "the companionship of a fellow Christian . . . is an unspeakable gift of God." This gift is "easily disregarded and trodden underfoot by those who have the gift every day." Dietrich Bonhoeffer, *Life Together*, trans. John W. Doberstein (New York, NY: Harper & Row, 1954), 20.

[13.] *Nutrition for Dummies*, 101–02.

[14] N.T. Wright, *Simply Christian: Why Christianity Makes Sense* (San Francisco, CA: HarperSanFrancisco, 2006): 149.

[15] *Nutrition for Dummies*, 126–30.

[16] Ibid., 84–5.

[17] It's easy to remember the difference this way: LDLs are "lousy"; HDLs are "happy."

ENDNOTES

[18] "Dietary Fats: Know Which Types to Choose," *http://mayoclinic.com/health/fat/ NU00262*, 2007.

[19] Small amounts of trans fats are naturally found in the food products of ruminant animals such as cows, sheep, and goats. These trans fats may not have the same harmful effect on our bodies as trans fats made from the hydrogenation process. "Ask the Experts," *University of California, Berkeley, Wellness Letter*, November 2008, 7. For a discussion see "Naturally occurring trans fats," *www.tfx.org.uk/page62.html*.

[20] For a discussion of unhealthy fats see "Solid Fats" at *mypyramid.org*, "Inside the Pyramid," "Discretionary Calories."

[21] Jesus often went to the synagogue to worship. The early believers met together regularly for worship and fellowship.

[22] H.G.M. Williamson, *Ezra, Nehemiah*, vol. 16, *Word Biblical Commentary*, ed. David A. Hubbard and Glenn W. Barker (Waco, TX: Word Books, 1985), xxxvii–xxxix; 288.

[23] Ibid. The assembled people included "men and women and all who were able to understand" (Nehemiah 8:2).

[24] John Ortberg, *God Is Closer Than You Think* (Grand Rapids, MI: Zondervan, 2005), 77.

[25] Werner Foerster, "*semnos, semnotes*," *Theological Dictionary of the New Testament*, vol. 7: 191–3.

[26] Richard Carlson, *Easier Than You Think . . . Because Life Doesn't Have to Be So Hard: The Small Changes That Add Up to a World of Difference* (New York, NY: HarperCollins, 2005), 13–15.

[27] I made it a point to read the Harry Potter books so that I would know what was in them. When a mother asked, "Should I let my son read the Harry Potter books" or "Should I take my daughter to the Harry Potter movie"

I would suggest that they read the books or go to the movie together. Then they could talk about the issues of witchcraft and magic as well as the human problems they share with the characters in the story. It is important to help our children learn to be discerning about what they see and read.

[28] See mypramidmoms. From the *mypramid.gov* homepage, click "Pregnancy & Breastfeeding" on the left.

[29] Eric Berne, the author of *Games People Play,* discussed a similar habit he called "trading stamps." People used to get Green Stamps with purchases. The stamps were pasted in a book and could be redeemed for a premium. In Berne's analogy, "stamps" are the slights we perceive from others. When we save enough stamps against someone else we feel entitled to "redeem" the stamps with anger against the offender.

[30] *Giving—the sacred art: Creating a Lifestyle of Generosity* © 2008 Lauren Tyler Wright, 68. Permission granted by SkyLight Paths Publishing, P.O. Box 237, Woodstock, VT 05091 *www.skylightpaths.com.*

[31] There are different approaches to the tithe. I tithe on my net income and any money I receive. I give offerings over and above my tithe. I am peaceful with this approach and I believe that it pleases God.

[32] Brennan Manning, *The Importance of Being Foolish: How to Think Like Jesus* (New York: HarperSanFrancisco, 2005), 168.

[33] For example, *Nutrition for Dummies* has a section describing how vitamins work together (p. 128).

[34] See "Food Synergy: Nutrients That Work Better Together" by Elaine Magee, *http://www.webmd.com/food-recipes/features/food-synergy-nutrients-that-work-better-together,* 2004.

ENDNOTES

[35] *Healthy Weight for EveryBody* (Rochester, MN: Mayo Clinic, 2005), 65–6.

Pray-as-you-go quotation: *pray-as-you-go.org*, Jesuit Media Initiatives, London, 2008.

To order additional copies of this title call:
1-877-421-READ (7323)
or please visit our Web site at
www.winepressbooks.com